CW00572362

PLEASING LORD KRISHNA

The Art of INDIAN SWEETS

Krishna Priya Dasi

Published by Torchlight Publishing Inc.
Published simultaneously in the United States and Canada

Drawings by Krishna Priya Dasi
Edited by MadanMohanMohini Dasi and Gurubhakta Dasi
Design and layout by Mayapriya Dasi, Bookwrights
Photographs by Lila-sakti Dasi, Karen Heyda, and Krishna Priya Dasi

Library of Congress Cataloging-in-Publication Data

Dasi, Krishna Priya.
The art of Indian sweets : pleasing Lord Krishna / by Krishna Priya dasi.
p. cm.
Includes bibliographical references.
ISBN 978-0-9817273-7-0
1. Desserts—India. 2. Confectionery. 3. Cooking, Indic. 4. Cookbooks. I. Title.
TX773.D293 2011
641.8'60954—dc23
2011017174

Printed in Kolkata, India

For more information on preparing sweets contact the author
at krsnapriyad@hotmail.com

P.O. Box 52, Badger, CA, USA 93603 • Phone 1.595.337.2200 • Fax 1.559.337.2354
torchlightpublishing@yahoo.com www.torchlight.com

Dedication

To His Divine Grace A.C. Bhaktivedanta Swami Prabhupada
Founder-Acarya of the International Society for Krishna Consciousness
Who blessed us with this rare opportunity
To experience this transcendental art:
Cooking for Krishna, the Supreme Personality.

Sri Sri Radha Golokananda

Hillsborough, North Carolina

Sri Sri Radha Govinda Dev Ji, Jaipur

Radharani carries sweets to Krishna,
The sweetest Lord of Sri Vrindavan dham.
She cooks 56 bhoga with pure devotion
To please Her most beloved Shyam.

Contents

Acknowledgments

I offer my heartfelt gratitude to my mother, Srimati Maina Devi Jeendgar, for inspiring and teaching me traditional Indian cooking in a simple way.

I humbly express my gratitude to my spiritual master, His Holiness Lokanath Swami, for his kind blessings upon my endeavor to write this cookbook.

My special thanks to my sisters, Sunita Agarwal and Vandana Agarwal, and my mother-in-law, Nancie Rosenberg for their encouragement.

It is difficult to find proper words to express my thanks to Madan MohanMohini dasi for devoting her time and full attention toward editing and writing articles for this cookbook even though she is fully engaged in devotional service.

I really like to express my gratitude to mother Gurubhakta for the final editing of this book and helping me in many different ways.

I am very thankful to Lila-sakti dasi and Karen Heyda who spent hours and hours to take photographs of my preparations. And special thanks to mother Krishna Priya for taking the photo of Sri Sri Golokananda for "Cooking for Krishna" (pg. 14). She has dedicated her whole life to serving Sri Sri Radha Golokananda with all purity and sincerity.

My special thanks to Mayapriya dasi for designing this book. She is very talented in this field and is such a kind soul to take the time to discuss so many details with me.

I am very thankful to Krishna Kumari dasi for taking time to explain traditional Indian cooking.

My gratitude to Shant Atma dasi and Preeti dasi for testing and being an impartial judge of my recipes.

I am very thankful to all who shared their recipes with me.

My special thanks to Adwaita Candra prabhu from Torchlight Publishing for being so responsive to my inquiries about my cookbook.

Above all, my deepest gratitude goes to the Supreme Personality of Godhead, Lord Krishna, for allowing me to try to do a little devotional service although I have no qualifications.

A Humble Request

Sri Vrindavan dham is also known as Goloka dham which means 'the land of the cows'. In the Vedic culture, the cow is considered to be like the mother because she gives us milk, a most important food. Lord Krishna, 'The Supreme Personality of Godhead' Himself, worshiped cows and personally took care of them very nicely to teach the world about the importance of taking care of cows. Lord Krishna is also known as Nanda go dhan rakhwala which means the protector of His father, Nanda baba's, cows.

Unfortunately, the situation of mother cow is extremely intense nowadays. In India they are abandoned from their homes when they become old and no longer give milk. As a result they are left unprotected to wander in the streets without food, water and shelter. They become victims of slaughterhouses and, as in the West, they are used for food.

Seeing this made me think very deeply that the goal of human life is not just for our personal gratification or for fulfilling our own needs or comforts, but it is for rising above selfishness and for doing something for the welfare of other living entities. Service to mother cow is always beneficial as she is very dear to Lord Krishna.

Fortunately, I got the chance to stay in Goloka Vrindavan dham from December, 2006 to March, 2007 with my husband Gopal Prabhu. It was a great blessing to meet Kurma Rupa Prabhu in Vrindavan dham because he has dedicated his life to take care of the local cows through his organization, Care for Cows. He adopts sick and old cows and arranges food, shelter and medical care for them though he faces many challenges.

My humble request to all of you is to spare some of your time and money to help mother cow. If you get a chance to visit Vrindavan dham, please visit Care for Cows and donate some money to this transcendental organization. Sending a donation from home is very easy. Go to www.careforcows.org and send your donation through PayPal or with a credit card.

May cows stay in front of me; may cows stay behind me; may cows stay on both sides of me. May I always reside in the midst of cows. —Hari Bhakti Vilas 16.252

Thank you very much. Hare Krishna.

Krishna Priya Dasi

Krishna Priya Dasi

56 Bhoga

56 bhoga means fifty-six preparations made for the Supreme Personality of Godhead, Sri Krishna. It is always an amazing experience for any devotee to cook this many preparations.

I was very fortunate to be raised in Jaipur, India under the shelter of Sri Sri Radha Govinda Dev Ji, Srila Rupa Goswami's original Deities. There is a very popular festivity at Their temple which is known as 56 bhoga jhanki (darshan). Anyone can go to see their beloved Lordships surrounded by traditional Vedic preparations. The recipes in this book are many of those same sweets that are offered on that special festival day; the day that I would meditate on how Sri Sri Radha Govinda Dev Ji were pleased by Their devotees' devotion.

I always felt that the devotees who cooked for the temple Deities were very fortunate, but I never thought that I would share the same fortune! I too received this great opportunity by the mercy of His Divine Grace A.C. Bhaktivedanta Swami Prabhupada. He established temples for Lord Krishna all around the world and gave a chance to those who were not born in Brahmana or Goswami families to cook for the Deities. It has definitely been a very inspiring experience for me to cook for Sri Sri Radha Golokananda at New Goloka in NC, USA. Although Lord Krishna has different names in different places, the fortune is the same.

Though my tiny efforts may be full of faults, they will become useful if some fortunate souls will cook these sweets for our sweetest Lord Krishna.

Hare Krishna.
Your servant,

Krishna Priya Dasi

Krishna Priya Dasi

Cooking for Krishna

Cooking is an art and one of the most wonderful ways to please someone. This art becomes transcendental and therefore meaningful if one cooks for The Supreme Personality of Godhead, Sri Krishna, 'the reservoir of all pleasure'. I have had many pleasant experiences in the art of cooking for Krishna, although I have had to face some seemingly impossible challenges in my life, due to my physical limitations.

I was born in Rajasthan, India, and was raised in Jaipur, the capital of Rajasthan. The land of Sri Sri Radha Govinda Dev Ji. I was born with a disability and as a result of this, have had heavy challenges with my bones as well as the rest of my physical structure. I also stand less than four feet tall. Because of all this, I was unable to go to school like the other girls and had to stay at home with my mother. While there, I would watch her very carefully as she cooked; she cooked three times a day. Her style was very simple. She didn't use many ingredients and used only a few steps to prepare something – and the tastes were always wonderful. My mother was always very protective of me and although I had an intense desire to cook, I was scared to ask her because I was sure she wouldn't let me – I was barely 11 years old. However, when she went out one time, I tried to imitate her cooking. Upon her return, she was very surprised but also upset as something could have happened in her absence. After that she allowed me to cook in her presence, and it was at that point that cooking became an everyday activity for me. Needless to say, I was very happy. A little while later I went to a cooking school in Jaipur, and although I was the youngest student in the class, I was able to earn a diploma.

Several years later, in 1988, I had some connection with Srila Prabhupada's movement, 'ISKCON'. One devotee from the New Delhi temple, Jitamitra prabhu, helped me on the devotional path and introduced me to His Holiness Lokanath Swami from whom I took initiation in 1992. My godsister, Prasanta Devi Dasi, had encouraged me to offer my food to Lord Krishna and when I did so, I felt I had received special blessings from the Lord. I never thought, however, that one day I would be able to cook for the Deities in an ISKCON temple.

By Lord Krishna's and my spiritual master's arrangement, in 1996 I moved to New Goloka in Hillsborough, NC, USA after marrying Gopal Prabhu. Just a few days after my arrival, one devotee from the temple asked me to help her roll besan laddu. It was my first time in the Deities' kitchen and I felt ecstatic! After that, several devotees asked me to regularly help roll sweets for the Deities, 'Sri Sri Radha Golokananda'. I so much desired to personally cook traditional Indian sweets for the Deities, especially sweets from Rajasthan, but it was difficult in the temple kitchen – everything was huge! After a few months, my husband hired someone to build a kitchen in my home which was suitable for my size and I was then able to make sweets as a regular service. I began to cook complicated Indian sweets and realized I needed to simplify the methods. From then on I started to write my own recipes. I received a lot of appreciation and encouragement from the devotees and visitors but I never thought I would write a cookbook.

Some years passed and in 2005 I had to undergo major brain surgery in India and almost died. But my life was saved in a miraculous way by the mercy of Lord Krishna and His devotees. During my recovery period from this long and intense illness, I often thought that had I left my body, all my recipes would have been lost. Upon my return to New Goloka after the surgery, I concluded that I should compile them into a cookbook because I wanted to share with others how cooking for Krishna is such a wonderful experience. To this day, I still struggle while cooking because my bones are weak and because my condition worsened after the brain surgery. But these challenges do not bother me when I start to cook for Krishna; I always experience inner satisfaction.

It is difficult for me to walk from my house to the temple to deliver the sweets I make for the deities. I often stumble along the way. Sometimes I have to sit down and rest. The distance seems like many miles to me due to my physical disability, though my home is only a few minutes walking distance from the temple. Still, I must say that while I carry the sweets to the temple, I feel unlimitedly happy, a feeling that cannot be compared to all the wealth in the three worlds.

Anyone can attain this transcendental happiness. The only requirements are desire and determination, and the mercy of Lord Krishna and His devotees. His Divine Grace A.C. Bhaktivedanta Swami Prabhupada has blessed us with the opportunity to cook for Krishna through his ISKCON (Hare Krishna) movement. It is never too late to start on our journey towards inner peace and happiness, and we can achieve this destination by following in Srila Prabhupada's and his followers' footsteps in cooking for Krishna.

I have tried to write this cookbook by following my mother's style and just as she cooked in a simple way, I, too, tried to write these recipes so they would be easy to follow. I also remember that some Rajasthani preparations that my grandmother used to cook were lost because they were not written down and therefore felt that I should finish many cookbooks as soon as possible because time is flying by and we are reaching our end very quickly. I know that there are sure to be mistakes, so I would very much appreciate it if you were to let me know of any corrections and comments you may have. I pray for your increased enthusiasm to cook for Krishna. Thank you very much.

Hare Krishna.

Your servant

Krishna Priya Dasi

Krishna Priya Dasi

How to Offer Food to Lord Krishna

As I am writing this, I am remembering when my husband and I went to visit my family for my mother's 85th birthday celebration; my family had planned a big party for her. One of the many special things they did was to have all of her favorite foods for dinner the night of the party. Needless to say, she was delighted and, of course, very happy to be with all of her family members and friends. So, we can see how, when we love someone, we want to share with or offer to them those things that they like the most.

And so, it is the same principle in cooking and offering to Krishna, the Supreme Personality and Enjoyer, the Lord in everyone's heart. As we show our love and devotion for Him by preparing those foodstuffs that He likes, He is pleased. This is called bhakti-yoga or the yoga of devotion. Krishna is the reservoir of all pleasure and as His parts and parcels we also experience spiritual happiness when He is pleased. Just as when water is poured on the root of the tree, all the leaves are nourished. Whatever we offer to Him becomes sanctified food or prasadam, Krishna's mercy, and we become spiritually and materially satisfied. We become free from all past karmic reactions and the body becomes immunized from all contamination of material nature, just as when there is an epidemic disease, an antiseptic vaccine protects a person from the illness. The reactions for not offering one's food are not only impediments to one's progress on the path of self-realization, but one's sinful reactions continue to increase as one continues to act as the enjoyer. As Krishna states in the Bhagavad-gita, 9.26-28: "If one offers Me with love and devotion a leaf, a flower, fruit or water, I will accept it. Whatever you do, whatever you eat, whatever you offer or give away, and whatever austerities you perform—do that, O son of Kunti, as an offering to Me. In this way you will be freed from bondage to work and its auspicious and inauspicious results. With your mind fixed on Me in this principle of renunciation, you will be liberated and come to Me." Lord Krishna also says in 3.13, "The devotees of the Lord are released from all kinds of sins because they eat food which is offered first for sacrifice. Others who prepare food for personal sense enjoyment verily eat only sin." Srila Prabhupada states in the purport, "...Others who prepare food for self or sense gratification are not only thieves but also the eaters of all kinds of sins. How can a person be happy if he is both a thief and sinful? It is not possible..." These points are worthy of consideration, for without adhering to such principles, there will be no peace or happiness in this world.

Many of you who use this cookbook may already know the process for offering, but for those who don't, here are some important guidelines:

~ As cleanliness is next to Godliness, keep your kitchen and clothing clean while cooking.

~ Don't taste anything until after it has been offered to Lord Krishna.

~ Try to think of Krishna while cooking.

~ Strictly avoid using meat, fish or eggs. Lord Krishna does not accept non-vegetarian items. He also does not accept onions, garlic and mushrooms so we do not use these in cooking.

~ Keep a special plate, bowls, cup and spoon for offerings and keep them separately from your eating utensils.

~ When making the plates for the offering, place some of what you have cooked into the bowls along with a cup of water or something to drink. Place the spoon on the plate.

~ If you are offering to Visnu tattva (Lord Krishna and Lord Caitanya, etc.), put a Tulasi leaf on each preparation.

~ You may offer to Krishna or God as you know Him by preparing an altar in a clean place in your home. You should make a curtain that you can close when you make an offering and while Lord Krishna eats. You can place three pictures on the altar: on the left, one of Srila Prabhupada, the spiritual master and founder-acarya (teacher) of the International Society for Krishna Consciousness, (if initiated by someone other than Srila Prabhupada, you would place that picture of your spiritual master to the left of Srila Prabhupada's and if not yet initiated, you would just have Srila Prabhupada's picture). The spiritual master is God's representative and it is through him that Krishna receives offerings. In the middle, place a picture of Lord Chaitanya (Krishna appearing as a devotee) and His associates who appeared 500 years ago in W. Bengal, India and on the right, one of Radha and Krishna. These pictures are available through www.krishna.com and www.krishnaculture.com or your nearest Hare Krishna center.

~You may say the following prayers, chant the Hare Krishna mantra or just ask the Lord to accept your offering. Each of the following four mantras should be recited three times. The English translations do not have to be spoken but have been provided so that you may understand the meaning of the Sanskrit mantras. The most important aspect in cooking and offering your food is your love and devotion.

1. nama om vishnu-padaya krishna-presthaya bhutale
   srimate bhaktivedanta-svamin iti namine

"I offer my respectful obeisances unto His Divine Grace A.C. Bhaktivedanta Swami Prabhupada, who is very dear to Lord Krishna, having taken shelter at His lotus feet."

2. namas te sarasvate deve gaura-vani-pracharine
   nirvishesha-shunyavadi-paschatya-desha tarine

"Our respectful obeisances unto you, O spiritual master, servant of Sarasvati Goswami. You are kindly preaching the message of Lord Chaitanya and delivering the Western countries, which are filled with impersonalism and voidism.

3. namo maha-vadanyaya krishna-prema-pradaya te
   krishnaya krishna-chaitanya-namne gaura-tvishe namaha

"I offer my respectful obeisances unto the Supreme Lord Sri Krishna Chaitanya, who is more magnanimous than any other incarnation, even Krishna Himself, because He is bestowing freely what no one else has ever given – pure love of Krishna."

4. namo-brahmanya-devaya go brahmana hitaya cha
   jagad-hitaya krishnaya govindaya namo namaha

"I offer my respectful obeisances to the Supreme Absolute Truth, Krishna, who is the well-wisher of the cows and the brahmanas as well as the living entities in general. I offer my repeated obeisances to Govinda [Krishna], who is the pleasure reservoir for all the senses."

If you like, you can also chant the following mantra, called the maha-mantra, or great mantra, several times:

Hare Krishna, Hare Krishna
Krishna Krishna, Hare Hare
Hare Rama, Hare Rama
Rama Rama, Hare Hare

There are many practical benefits from chanting this maha-mantra and the following explains some of them:

Lord Caitanya Mahaprabhu recommended: ceto-darpana-marjanam [Cc. Antya 20.12]. Marjana means "cleanse," and darpana means "mirror." The heart is a mirror. It is like a camera. Just as a camera takes all kinds of pictures of days and nights, so also our heart takes pictures and keeps them in an unconscious state. Psychologists know this. The heart takes so many pictures, and therefore it becomes covered. We do not know when it has begun, but it is a fact that because there is a material contact, our real identity is covered. Therefore ceto-darpana-marjanam: one has to cleanse his heart.... Simply chant Hare Krishna. It is the easiest and most sublime process. This is recommended, practical, and authorized. So take it. Accept it in any condition of life. Chant. There is no expenditure, there is no loss. We are not chanting a secret. No. It is open. And by chanting you will cleanse your heart.

One can directly perceive the results of chanting—transcendental pleasure and purification. It is said that the execution of devotional service is so perfect that one can perceive the results directly. This direct result is actually perceived, and we have practical experience that any person who is chanting the holy names of Krishna (Hare Krishna, Hare Krishna, Krishna Krishna, Hare Hare Hare Rama, Hare Rama, Rama Rama, Hare Hare) in course of time feels some transcendental pleasure and very quickly becomes purified of all material contamination. This is actually seen.

Bhagavad-gita As It Is Chapter 9, verse 2:

"The Brhan Naradiya Purana states about the maha-mantra: 'My dear King, although Kali-yuga is full of faults, there is still one good quality about this age. It is that simply by chanting the Hare Krishna maha-mantra, one can become free from material bondage and be promoted to the transcendental kingdom.' (Srimad Bhagavatam Canto 12, Chapter 3, verse 51)

harer nama harer nama
harer namaiva kevalam
kalau nasty eva nasty eva
nasty eva gatir anyatha

"In this age of quarrel and hypocrisy the only means of deliverance is chanting the holy name of the Lord. There is no other way. There is no other way. There is no other way."

~ After 10-15 minutes, you may remove the offering and open the curtains. Place the offered foodstuffs either back in their pots or into a separate container and wash and dry the plate, etc. You, your friends and family members may now enjoy spiritual karma free food. Hare Krishna.

MadanMohanMohini dasi

Prasadam Distribution

"Somehow or other everyone can manage to perform such a yajna (sankirtana) and distribute prasadam to the people in general. That is quite sufficient for this age of Kali. The Hare Krishna movement is based on this principle: chant the Hare Krishna mantra at every moment, both inside and outside of the temples, and, as far as possible, distribute prasadam. This process can be accelerated with the help of the state administrators and those who are producing the country's wealth. Simply by liberal distribution of prasadam and sankirtana, the whole world can become peaceful and prosperous". (Srimad Bhagavatam 4.12.10).

From this statement of Srila Prabhupada's, we can see that distributing prasadam, that food which becomes sanctified by offering it to the Lord, is very important for the upliftment of society; both the distributor and receiver are benefitted spiritually. Certainly, it is one of the easiest and blissful ways to give someone Krishna consciousness. When we understand that prasadam (whether sanctified foodstuffs or other paraphernalia of the Lord) is the mercy of and is non-different from Lord Krishna, we realize how wonderful it is to receive the Lord's remnants. But even more wonderful and satisfying is giving this mercy to others; one of the six symptoms of love is giving and receiving prasadam.

Everyone loves something good to eat, especially something homemade. There's a saying that the way to one's heart is through their stomach and certainly prasadam does just that; it will always touch people's hearts. Prasadam purifies the heart of the taker and Srila Prabhupada explains that when one honors these sanctified foodstuffs, even unknowingly, then he is guaranteed a human birth in his next life and continues where he left off in his previous life. This goes for animals, insects – anyone. It is stated in the Caitanya-caritamrta: "In the Hare Krishna movement the chanting of the Hare Krishna maha-mantra, the dancing in ecstasy and the eating of remnants of food to the Lord are very important. One may be illiterate or incapable of understanding the philosophy, but if he partakes of these three items, he will certainly be liberated without delay." There is one story, amongst so many, that I would like to narrate. For many years, we have made pakoras and tomato chutney for the Stokes Stomp, a local event. We have made so many friends, enhanced our relationship with existing friends and have become the favorite booth that many say they wait all year long to come back to! Some tell us that it is the only thing they will eat at the Stomp! One such person, Sara, the woman who began the Stomp over 35 years ago, became an acquaintance of mine through her love of pakoras and chutney. She would always come and talk with me, inquire about vegetarianism and tell me that she had a health problem from her poor eating habits. One year, I was wondering why I hadn't seen her and was feeling her absence. I then saw a banner honoring her work for the Stomp and found out she had passed away. Needless to say, I felt sadness; she was a very sweet person. But, then I thought about how she had been so attached to the pakoras and chutney and realized that because of her contact with prasadam, she was now certainly in a much better position and, from this thought, I felt great relief and happiness. In the Caitanya-caritamrta, Srila Prabhupada explains, "Actually, by eating such maha-prasadam one is freed of all the contaminations of the material condition."

It is good to remember how Srila Prabhupada, despite the lack of facility, cooked and distributed prasadam to those on the Jaladuta, the boat he took on his way over to the States. So, we too can distribute prasadam practically anywhere and in any circumstance; it helps people feel at ease and is a great way to make friends. To get started, you can make something that is visually acceptable by everyone (cookies, for example). Then, when you go somewhere, you can give them to those you meet. This often sparks people's curiosity and they will ask questions about Krishna consciousness and may even take a book. If you work, you can always keep something on your desk for others to take. My husband and I always distribute the maha burfi from our Deities, Sri Sri Radha-Syamasundara, to everyone who comes to our door and to the many people we meet. We always invite people to our home for prasadam. As a result, we are very often invited to participate in different events, attend college and school classes as well as give cooking demonstrations. So many times we have experienced that people also ask for our recipes, but when they try to cook that preparation, they come back and tell us that they followed the recipe exactly but theirs just didn't taste the same! That always gives us the opportunity to tell them about our two secret ingredients: Bhakti for the Supreme Person and offering our food to Him.

As Srila Prabhupada explains, "Ours is not a dry philosophy—simply talk and go away. No. We distribute prasadam, very sumptuous prasadam. In every temple we offer prasadam to anyone who comes. In each and every temple we already have from fifty to two hundred devotees, and outsiders also come and take prasadam. So prasadam distribution is a symptom of the guru. Prasadam is not ordinary food, because prasadam has the potency to make us gradually become spiritualized. Therefore it is said that realization of God begins with the tongue. By engaging our tongue in the service of the Lord, then we realize God. So what is that engagement of the tongue? We chant the holy name of the Lord, and we take His prasadam. Then, by these two methods, we become God realized. You don't have to be very highly educated or be a philosopher, a scientist, or a rich man to realize God. If you just sincerely engage your tongue in the service of the Lord, you will realize Him. It's so simple. That's why the guru introduces this prasadam program. And when the guru sees that prasadam distribution is going on, he is very pleased." Such a simple way to please our spiritual master and Krishna!

In closing, once, after a lecture, a disciple asked Srila Prabhupada what happens if a devotee gives someone a little morsel of prasadam, such as the "simply wonderfuls". Srila Prabhupada replied, "Then that is wonderful. Simply wonderful! He has not tasted such a wonderful sweet in his life. Therefore, you give him a simply wonderful, and because he is eating that wonderful sweet, one day he will come to your temple and become wonderful. Therefore it is simply wonderful. So go on distributing these simply wonderfuls." He thought for a moment, and then said, "Your philosophy is simply wonderful, the prasadam is simply wonderful, you are simply wonderful, and your Krishna is simply wonderful. The whole process is simply wonderful." The devotees responded, "Srila Prabhupada is simply wonderful!" It is said in the Guruvastakam, "yasya prasadad bhagavat prasada". It is only by the mercy of the spiritual master that one can receive the mercy of Krishna." Hare Krishna.

MadanMohanMohini dasi

The Wisdom Behind Vegetarianism

Most of us are familiar with the old adage, "You are what you eat". Does this mean that if I eat a carrot, I'm a carrot? No, of course not. So then, what does this really mean and what relevance does this have to our lives?

The Vedic literature, particularly the Bhagavad-gita As It Is by His Divine Grace A.C. Bhaktivedanta Swami Prabhupada, explains that there are three modes of material nature – goodness, passion and ignorance – which influence and control every aspect of our lives. From this influence, we become conditioned or accustomed to think and act in certain ways; we will even prefer eating certain foods. For example, if we are influenced by the mode of goodness, we will eat foods such as vegetables, fruits, grains, nuts, milk and milk products. From eating these things, we will experience happiness, longevity and better health and will perceive things clearly. If we eat foods that are too bitter, too sour and hot, we are influenced by the mode of passion. However, if we are influenced by the mode of ignorance, we will eat things like meat, fish and eggs – decomposed foods – and the end result will be lethargy, misery, disease and we will not be able to see things as they are.

One of the very basic points in the 'Bhagavad-gita As It Is' is that every living entity is an eternal, spiritual soul, a fragmental part of Krishna or God; the body is just a temporary covering. Krishna sees and loves all of His parts and parcels – humans, animals, birds, insects, vegetation, etc. – equally. Although all living entities have intelligence to different degrees, Krishna gives only us, the human beings, higher intelligence to understand who we are, who He is, and what our relationship to Him is, as well as the intelligence to understand what is right and wrong and to act accordingly. Also, all beings are given a quota; animals are sanctioned to kill and eat other living entities, but humans are not. He explains what is acceptable in the ninth chapter of Bhagavad-gita As It Is, "If one offers Me with love and devotion a leaf, a flower, fruit or water, I will accept it." So, it is simple – we only need to change our consciousness to understand that everything is coming from Krishna or God, and we should use everything in connection with Him, as well as offer our food in love to Him. It is a simple process and if we please Krishna, we too, will become satisfied.

The following are some of the differences between the body of a human being and that of an animal:

1. The human's intestinal tract is 6 times his body length, but that of the carnivore's is only 3 times longer so that the decaying meat can be quickly digested and excreted. Because the human's is longer, the meat has a much longer way to travel in order to be digested and therefore sits and decays causing disease.
2. The hydrochloric acid in the stomach of a meat-eater is much stronger than in the body of a human which allows the carnivore the ability to digest flesh more easily.
3. The difference between human teeth and those of a carnivore's show that the human's are meant for chewing, not for tearing flesh. If you've ever watched a dog eat, he tears the meat and barely chews it before swallowing it.

   Because we know that there is much talk about following a vegetarian diet, we ask that if you are thinking about what you eat, please also consider these important health facts. They speak for themselves.

1. A vegetarian diet provides protection against chronic diseases such as cancer, cardiovascular disease and diabetes and is rich in health-promoting factors such as phytochemicals. Dr. Gary Fraser, Professor of Epidemiology at Loma Linda University, affirms that fruit, vegetables and fiber protect one against heart disease.
2. Vegetarian diets are generally lower in saturated fat and cholesterol.
3. It is suspected that meat-eaters are prime candidates for degenerative diseases such as arthritis and gout, etc.
4. Studies have shown that when an animal is slaughtered, waste products remain in the tissues of the animal and that is what gives the meat its stimulating flavor! Toxins such as uric acid and adrenaline are secreted into the bloodstream and muscles of the animal and the fear and struggle to escape death stimulates the secretion of hormones such as epinephrine, norepinephrine and steroids. In contrast, no edible plant has similar toxicity. When

the flesh of these animals is eaten, the human body has to work 15 times harder to get rid of the toxins although some toxins actually accumulate in each and every cell.

5. Pigs carry trichinosis bacteria that cling to the walls of the stomach and intestines and can be fatal. Beef and pork are highly acid-forming and release toxic poisons and microbes into the blood-stream; however, the white blood count (WBC) in the person who ingested the meat may not be sufficient to destroy these microbes and so toxic reactions set in.

6. Boric acid is widely used by food manufacturers to preserve fish, prawns and other crustaceans and this attacks the liver and brain causing fits and coma before the victim dies of liver damage. Fruits and vegetables, even if heavily sprayed, don't contain hormones, antibiotics and other drugs common in meat products. And the list goes on.

But people are not vegetarian just for health reasons; they also take into consideration the following economic and environmental factors:

1. A meat-centered diet is wasteful. For example, it takes 16 pounds of grain to feed each animal and from that animal, we get only 1 pound of meat. Those grains, instead, could be used to feed millions of people.

2. Another point is that the environment is destroyed; so many rivers and streams are polluted from run-off and sewage from slaughterhouses. Statistics for water usage for these animals is astounding.

3. Forests are being destroyed for grazing and this creates erosion problems as well as takes away the homes of so many helpless creatures. Is this right? Is this fair? If you consider that all living entities are eternal souls, are parts of God and have a right to live, then you will answer "no" to these questions.

4. A vegetarian diet is cheaper!

So now let's take a look at some moral reasons for becoming vegetarian. A non-vegetarian diet is a product of violence; a vegetarian diet is a compassionate diet as it causes less pain to others. All living entities have consciousness but just because some living entities' consciousness is not as developed as ours, does this give us the right to kill and eat them? They, too, have feelings. By not taking their lives, one actually shows respect to them, understanding that they also have a right to live according to God's plan. If we abhor the thought of someone killing and eating our family dog, why don't we feel the same about killing and eating a cow? And our young children. Their intelligence is not very developed; babies mostly eat and sleep just like the animals. They both have feelings and experience happiness and distress although they cannot express their feelings as we do. So, then what is the difference between killing and eating our children or killing and eating an animal?

"As you sow, so shall you reap." "Do unto others as you would have them do unto you." So many worthwhile statements and they all point to karma, the law of action and reaction. Whatever we do comes back on us. It's a scientific fact. So, if living entities have undergone suffering just so that we can eat (or even "sport") when there is ample space to grow food, then we, too, at some point, shall experience bad reactions from the pain those living entities have had to experience. This applies to whether we've directly participated in the slaughtering process or have indirectly participated through handling, purchasing, transporting, cooking the meat, etc. These are the laws of nature, the laws of God. How can we expect to have peace in this world if we are committing so much violence towards others? Leo Tolstoy wrote that by killing animals for food, "Man suppresses in himself, unnecessarily, the highest spiritual capacity – that of sympathy and pity towards living creatures like himself – and by violating his own feelings becomes cruel." He further states, "While our bodies are the living graves of murdered animals, how can we expect any ideal conditions on earth?" What goes around comes around.

We've spoken about animal killing, but what about taking the life of vegetables? Although there is very little killing when we harvest vegetables and fruits (the pear first ripens and then is picked, the wheat plant dies and then the grain is harvested), we do have to take the life of vegetables such as carrots, etc. You may ask, is there karma involved? Yes, there is karma, but it certainly is not as severe as when an animal is killed. So, what can we do about these actions and reactions? Can we become freed from this karma? The answer is yes.

Krishna explains in the 9th chapter of Bhagavad-gita As It Is, "Whatever you do, whatever you eat, whatever you offer or give away, and whatever austerities you perform – do that, O son of Kunti, as an offering to Me. In this way you will be freed from bondage to work and its auspicious and inauspicious results. With your mind fixed on Me in this principle of renunciation, you will be liberated and come to Me." Krishna also says in the third chapter, "The devotees of the Lord are released from all kinds of sins because they eat food which is offered first for sacrifice. Others, who prepare food for personal sense enjoyment, verily eat only sin." Simply put, Krishna says to offer everything acceptable to Him first and you will then become freed from all sinful reactions. He is providing everything for us, so why not offer everything in gratitude to Him first?

Following a vegetarian diet is not as difficult as you may think. This cookbook is amongst many which will teach you how to prepare wonderful dishes in a simple way and then offer them to the Lord. Oh, yes, one more thing. Not only is being a vegetarian much cheaper, but you can even grow your own! So, why not begin a more compassionate way of life through a vegetarian diet and promote peace within and without.

MadanMohanMohini dasi

Notes and Measurements

1. Cleanliness is very important. It is essential to take a shower, put on clean clothes and tie your hair back when you cook for the Deities.

2. Although I've mentioned the three or four different pans I use for cooking, you can use any suitable pan. It is also good to rinse your pans before cooking.

3. I always listen to kirtans and bhajans when I cook. I find that spiritual sound vibration is very potent as it helps to fix the consciousness.

4. There are generally two types of sugar which are most often used in India: white sugar and powdered sugar which I use in most of my recipes. You can try organic, brown, or raw sugar, etc., though the sweetness of these sugars is different from the white and powdered sugars.

5. In India, silver foil is used a lot to decorate sweets. I have however met several people from Jaipur who told me that silver foil is not pure vegetarian. In Jaipur, I once saw that a man was pounding silver between two layers of animal leather to make the foil. Since seeing this, I don't use silver foil for my sweets. Although there may be purely processed silver foil for sweets, I don't take the chance when I cook for the Deities.

6. If a mixture is too dry to roll the sweets, then you can add extra melted ghee or unsalted butter. If a mixture is too moist to roll the sweets, then you can add ground nuts or put it in the freezer for a few minutes.

7. If the instant, non-fat dry milk powder has lumps, sift or blend it. This is especially important when making gulab jamuns.

I am using a teaspoon, tablespoon, and cup to measure the ingredients as well as ml, liter and gallon to measure liquid ingredients. I am only using the American cup and spoon measurements in this book.

TEASPOON: The American, Australian and British teaspoon all hold approximately 5 ml.

TABLESPOON: The American tablespoon holds 14.2 ml, the Australian tablespoon holds 20 ml and the British tablespoon holds 17.7 ml.

CUP: The American and British cup hold 240 ml and the Australian cup holds 250 ml.

TEMPERATURE: The temperature for deep frying is given first in Fahrenheit then in Celsius. A cooking thermometer is required to measure the temperature of the ghee or oil.

How to Decorate Sweets

I often draw designs on my sweets which is fun and a wonderful way to make them even more attractive. I use good quality, liquid food coloring that is available in four colors: Yellow, red, green and blue. I mix red and yellow color to make orange color.

I use # 0 round brushes that are made from synthetic hair; I am very careful to not purchase brushes made from animal hair. I usually decorate sweets that have a white and smooth surface like burfi, sandesh or sattu. But you can always experiment with your decorations and colors. Some designs to decorate sweets can be found below

Ghee

Ghee is one of the main ingredients in traditional Indian cooking and is used in most of the recipes in this cookbook. To make ghee, do the following:

Preparation and cooking time: about 40-50 minutes
Makes: 1 2/3 cups of ghee

1 lb. unsalted butter

1. Cut the butter into medium-sized pieces and place in a heavy-bottomed, 3-quart saucepan.
2. Cook over medium heat until the butter is melted and the surface is covered with white foam. From time to time you will need to remove the solids or foam that accumulates on the surface of the butter.
3. Reduce the heat as low as possible and simmer the butter uncovered and undisturbed until the solids have settled on the bottom of the saucepan. When the liquid is clear and golden, it has become ghee and is finished. Immediately remove the pot from the heat or the ghee may turn brown which means it has burned. This process will take 35-40 minutes.
4. Allow the ghee to cool and settle down for 10-12 minutes. Take a container that is large enough to hold the ghee and place a metal sieve on top of it. Place a muslin cloth over the sieve.
5. Pour the ghee into the cloth-lined sieve and strain it. The solids will remain in the cloth and you can use them for vegetables, soups, or bread spread.

Paneer - Chenna

Homemade cheese

Paneer is the main ingredient in many Bengali sweets. It is also a substitute for mawa (cooked down milk) used in Indian sweets. I mostly use buttermilk as a curdling agent to make paneer, but you can try other ingredients like lemon juice, yogurt, or citric acid.

Preparation and cooking time: about 30 minutes
Makes: 10 oz. (285 g or 11/2 cups) paneer

8 cups (2 liters or half gallon) whole milk
1½ cups or as required buttermilk or 4 tablespoons lemon juice

1. Stirring occasionally, heat the milk over medium heat in a heavy-bottomed, 6-quart stockpot until the milk starts to boil. This will take about 20 minutes. While stirring, slowly pour the buttermilk or lemon juice into the milk. The milk will separate into yellow-greenish whey and white curds or paneer. If the whey is not clear, then add some extra buttermilk or lemon juice.

3. Line a colander with two layers of cheesecloth and place it over another container to collect the whey. The whey can be used for cooking. Remove the large lumps of paneer with a slotted spoon and place them in the colander. Gently pour the whey with the remaining small lumps of paneer into the cloth-lined colander.

4. After the liquid has drained from the paneer, gather the four corners of the cheesecloth and tie them tightly together. Hold it cold running water for 1 minute to rinse off the flavor of the buttermilk or lemon juice.

5. Place the paneer under a heavy weight to press out any remaining liquid for 30 to 40 minutes. The paneer will become firm and is now ready to use. (Some recipes require firm paneer and others do not.)

Note: The quantity of paneer depends upon the quality of the milk used.

Sweet Recipes

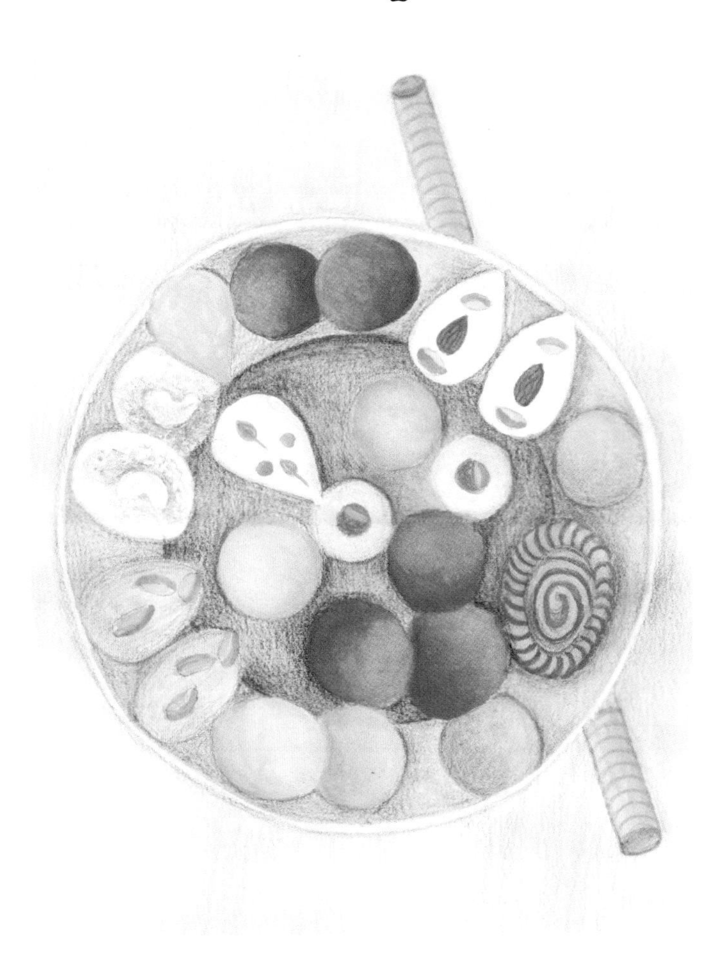

Whole Wheat Halva

I would like to share this special recipe that my mother used to make. It is a very common halva in Jaipur and is offered with roasted papadams. The combination of sweet halva with roasted, spicy papadams is quite interesting.

Preparation and cooking time: about 30 minutes
Serves: 4 to 6 persons

1 cup sugar
2 cups water
¾ cup ghee or unsalted butter
1 cup whole wheat flour

1. Place the sugar and water in a 2-quart saucepan and boil until the sugar dissolves. Cover it and on the lowest heat, allow the water to continue boiling.
2. Melt the ghee or butter in a 3-quart saucepan. Add the flour and stirring constantly, cook over medium heat for about 15 minutes or until the flour becomes light brown.
3. Turn the heat off and slowly pour the sugar water into the flour and stir.
4. The mixture will sputter but will absorb the water quickly. Turn the heat on low and continue to stir the halva until it becomes thick.
5. Offer the hot halva with roasted papadams to Lord Krishna.

Almond Halva

Almond halva is considered very opulent in Jaipur. It is cooked at home for when a very special guest comes to visit. So you can cook this for the most special person of all – Lord Krishna.

Preparation and cooking time: about 1 hour
Serves: 5 persons

1 cup almonds
1½ cups whole milk
¾ cup sugar
½ cup ghee or unsalted butter

1. Soak the almonds in boiling water in a covered container for 15 minutes. Rinse them under cold water and peel the skins off. In a food processor, grind the almonds and ¾ cup of milk to a fine paste.

2. Boil the remaining milk (¾ cup) with the sugar in a 2-quart saucepan. Partially cover and cook over the lowest heat so the milk continues to gently boil.

3. Melt the ghee or butter in a non-stick 3-quart saucepan and add the almond paste. Stir constantly over medium heat for about 20 minutes or until it changes color and the ghee or butter separates from the mixture.

4. Turn off the heat and carefully add the milk and sugar mixture as it tends to sputter.

5. Turn the heat on medium and stirring constantly, cook the mixture for 5-6 minutes or until the halva becomes thick.

6. Offer to Lord Krishna.

Dal Ka Halva

This halva is considered the tastiest halva in Rajasthan. Usually it is cooked during Holi (which falls on Gaura Purnima) and Diwali (festival of lights) and is offered to the Deities with dal kachories. My brother's wife, Sarita Jeendgar, cooks this halva on a wood stove and her halva is amazing!

Preparation and cooking time: about 1 hour
Serves: 6 to 8 persons

1 cup yellow split moong dal
1 cup ghee or unsalted butter
1½ cups (360 ml) milk
1¼ cups sugar
½ teaspoon cardamom powder
¼ teaspoon saffron

1. Soak the dal in water for 6-8 hours or overnight if you are going to cook in the morning.
2. Strain the dal and then rinse it under running water. In a food processor, grind dal to a thick paste by adding a little water.
3. Boil the milk, sugar, cardamom powder and saffron in a 2-quart saucepan. Partially cover and allow it to continue boiling over the lowest heat.

4. Melt the ghee or butter in a non-stick, 6-quart pan. Add the dal mixture and stir constantly over medium heat for about 30 minutes. Turn the heat down to low and cook 8-10 minutes more. Remove the pan from the heat and continuing to stir, slowly pour the sweet liquid into the cooked dal mixture. At first, the halva may sputter but will eventually absorb the liquid.

5. Cook halva on low heat until it becomes thick and fluffy. This will take 6-7 minutes.

6. Offer the hot halva along with dal kachories to Lord Krishna.

Chickpea Flour Halva

Although most ISKCON temples offer semolina halva to the Deities for breakfast, you can try this besan halva for a nice change.

Preparation and cooking time: about 30 minutes
Serves: 4 to 6 persons

2½ cups milk
¾ cup sugar
1 teaspoon cardamom powder
1 cup ghee or unsalted butter
1 cup chickpea flour
2 tablespoons sliced pistachios for garnish

1. Combine the milk, sugar and cardamom powder in a 2-quart saucepan and bring to a boil. Partially cover it and, on the lowest heat, allow the milk to continue boiling.

2. Melt ghee or butter in a non-stick, 3-quart saucepan. Add the chickpea flour and stirring constantly; cook the flour over medium heat until it turns light brown. It will take about 15 minutes.

3. Turn off the heat. Slowly pour the sweetened milk into the cooked chickpea flour and stir constantly. At first the mixture may sputter, but it will quickly absorb the milk.

4. Turn the heat on low and cook until the mixture becomes thick.

5. Garnish with the sliced pistachios.

6. Offer to Lord Krishna.

Buckwheat Flour Halva

In Vrindavan, on Ekadasi, my friend, Janaki dasi, gave me buckwheat halva. I liked it so much that even though I did not have the actual recipe, I made it for Radha-Golokananda when I returned. Here is the recipe which the devotees really liked.

Preparation and cooking time: about 30 minutes.
Serves: 5 persons

2 cups whole milk
2 tablespoons raisins
¾ cup sugar
½ cup ghee or unsalted butter
1 cup buckwheat flour

1. Boil the milk, sugar and raisins in a 2-quart saucepan. Partially cover the mixture and leave it on low so the milk gently boils.
2. Melt the ghee or butter in a non-stick, 3-quart saucepan. Add the flour and stirring constantly, cook for about 15 minutes over medium heat or until the ghee or butter separates from the mixture. Turn off the heat. Slowly pour in the sweetened milk and stir constantly. Be careful as the halva will sputter.
3. Turn the heat on low and stirring constantly, cook until the halva thickens.
4. Offer to Lord Krishna.

Carrot Halva

This halva is quite light compared to other halvas as it does not require a lot of sugar and ghee and is very nice to offer on Ekadasi.

Preparation and cooking time: about 30 minutes
Serves: 2 persons

2 cups (480 ml or ½ liter) whole milk
1 cup peeled, finely shredded carrots (3-4 medium-sized carrots)
¼ cup sugar
½ tablespoon ghee or unsalted butter

1. Using a thick-bottomed 3-quart saucepan, bring the milk to a boil. Add the shredded carrots. Stirring frequently, over moderately high heat, cook for about 15-20 minutes or until the halva thickens.
2. Add the sugar and ghee or unsalted butter. Stir constantly and cook for about 7-8 minutes so the mixture again thickens.
3. Offer to Lord Krishna.

Cashew and Coconut Halva

Once my husband, Gopal Prabhu, was joking that Ekadasi means feasting not fasting. To encourage the feasting, I decided to try making different Ekadasi halvas. This particular halva is very much appreciated by devotees in New Goloka.

Preparation and cooking time: about 35 minutes
Serves: 5 persons

1 cup cashews
½ cup dried, grated coconut
1½ cups (360 ml) whole milk
¾ cup sugar
½ cup ghee or unsalted butter

1. Grind the cashews and coconut in a food processor by adding as much milk as needed to make a fine paste (approximately ¾ cup milk). This will take about 2 minutes.

2. Boil the remaining milk (¾ cup) and sugar in a 2-quart saucepan. Partially cover it and leave it on the lowest heat so it continues to boil.

3. Melt the ghee or butter in a non-stick, 3-quart saucepan. Add the cashew and coconut paste and cook over medium heat for about 15 minutes. Turn the heat to low and stirring constantly, cook the halva for 7-8 minutes more.

4. Turn the heat off and continuing to stir, slowly pour the boiled milk and sugar in. Turn the heat on again and for about 5 minutes, cook the halva over medium heat until it becomes thick and floppy.

5. Offer the hot halva on this special day of 'Ekadasi' to Lord Hari, Who takes away all anxieties of this material life.

Lapsi

This is a traditional Rajasthani cereal which is usually offered in the wintertime.

Preparation and cooking time: about 45 minutes
Serves: 4 to 6 persons

½ cup ghee or unsalted butter
1 cup cracked wheat
3½ cups (840 ml) hot water
¾ cup jaggery
2 tablespoons chopped almonds

1. Melt the ghee or butter in a 3-quart saucepan. Add the cracked wheat and stirring constantly, cook over medium heat for about 7-8 minutes or until it becomes light brown.

2. Add the hot water and cover the pan. Stirring a few times, cook for about 12-15 minutes or until the water is absorbed and cracked wheat is cooked. You can use extra hot water if it is required.

3. Add the chopped almonds and jaggery. Cook until the jaggery is melted and the liquid is absorbed.

4. Offer to Lord Krishna.

Posh Khichadi

This sweet khichadi is a traditional Rajasthani preparation. It is offered with spicy dal pakoras to the Deities in almost all the temples in Jaipur during the month of Posh (January). Many temples organize big feasts for public distribution of this khichadi.

Preparation and cooking time: about 1 hour
Serves: 6 to 8 persons

½ cup rice
¼ cup yellow split moong dal
2 cups (480 ml) milk
2 cups (480 ml) water
2 tablespoons raisins
2 tablespoons chopped cashews
2 tablespoons chopped pistachios
½ teaspoon cardamom powder
¼ teaspoon saffron
1 cup sugar
2 tablespoons ghee

1. Soak the rice and dal together in water for 10-15 minutes. Strain the water and rinse the rice and dal under cold running water.

2. Mix the milk and water in a 3-quart saucepan. Bring to a boil and add the rice, dal and raisins. Stirring occasionally, cook for 20-25 minutes or until the liquid evaporates and the grains are cooked. Add the cashews, pistachios, cardamom powder, saffron and sugar and cook until the sugar water is evaporated. Add the ghee and mix well.

4. Offer to Lord Krishna.

Kesar Bhat

Kesar bhat is also known as "chashani ke chaval" in Jaipur. This yellow sweet rice is offered to the Deities in almost every home on Ramnavami.

Preparation and cooking time: about 40 minutes
Serves: 4 persons

½ cup basmati rice
5 cups (1200 ml) water
1 teaspoons turmeric
1 tablespoon ghee
4 whole cloves
½ cup sugar
2 tablespoons whole milk
1/3 teaspoon crushed cardamom
¼ teaspoon saffron
1 tablespoon sliced almonds
1 tablespoon sliced pistachios

1. Soak the rice in water for 10-15 minutes, then strain and rinse it under cold running water.

2. Boil 5 cups of water in a 6-quart stockpot. Add the turmeric and rice. Cook for about 15 minutes over medium heat making sure the grains are fully cooked. Strain the extra water.

3. Melt the ghee in a 3-quart saucepan and add the cloves. Cook for

2-3 minutes and then remove the cloves from the ghee. Add the sugar and milk. Stir constantly until the sugar dissolves, then add the cardamom powder and saffron and cook for 1-2 minutes more.

4. Add the cooked yellow rice; mix carefully so the rice does not break. Decorate with sliced almonds and pistachios.

5. Offer to Lord Krishna.

Panjiri

Panjiri is the special bhoga (preparation) offered in Rajasthan on Janmastami, the appearance day of Lord Krishna. All the temples and most of the householders of Jaipur offer this to their Deities on this day. Panjiri maha prasada is distributed to thousands of people at the Sri Sri Radha Govinda Dev Ji temple in Jaipur at midnight on Janmastami.

Preparation and cooking time: about 20 minutes
Serves: 4 to 6 persons

1 cup whole coriander seeds
1 tablespoon gond (edible gum available at Indian grocery stores)
2 tablespoons char magaz (cantaloupe seeds available at Indian grocery stores)
2 tablespoons chopped almonds
3 tablespoons melted ghee or unsalted butter
1/3 cup ground sugar
ghee for deep frying

1. Dry roast the coriander seeds in a pan over medium heat until they become brown. This will take about 5 minutes. Grind the browned seeds in a blender or spice grinder until they become a fine powder. This will take 2-3 minutes. Transfer to a mixing bowl.

2. Heat the ghee in a 2½" (6.5 cm) deep frying pan until the temperature reaches 300°F (148°C). Add the gond. It will puff and become about three times larger than it was originally. It will take about 2-3 minutes.

3. Add the char magaz, chopped almonds, fried gond, melted ghee or butter, ground sugar with the ground coriander seeds. Mix well.

4. Offer to Lord Krishna.

Note: I am using ground sugar instead of powdered sugar because powdered sugar generally contains cornstarch. (The sugar is ground in a blender or spice grinder). Corn is a grain and devotees fast from grains on Ekadasi, Janmastami and other special days.

Mithi Sevai

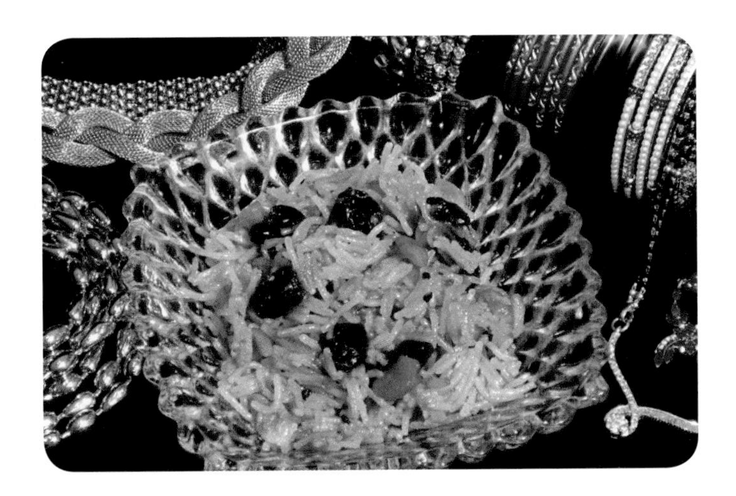

There is one festival named Teej in Rajasthan. Usually this festival honors young, unmarried girls. I still remember how my mother used to cook mithi sevai for this festival. There is also a procession organized on this day on the streets of Jaipur.

Preparation and cooking time: about 25 minutes
Serves: 2 to 3 persons

2 tablespoons ghee or unsalted butter
3 tablespoons chopped cashews
2 tablespoons raisins
1 cup vermicelli
1½ cups (360 ml) hot water
½ cup sugar
¼ teaspoon cardamom powder

1. Melt the ghee or butter in a 3-quart saucepan. Add the cashews and raisins and stirring constantly, cook over low heat for 2-3 minutes. Continue stirring and add the vermicelli, cooking for another 2-3 minutes.
2. Add the hot water and cover the saucepan. Cook over low heat until the liquid evaporates and the vermicelli is cooked. This will take 6-8 minutes. While cooking uncover the pan a few times and move the vermicelli around with wooden spatula so it does not stick.
3. Add the sugar and cardamom powder. Cook 5-7 minutes more or until the liquid evaporates.
4. Offer hot mithi sevai to Lord Krishna.

Mitha Poora

This is a traditional Rajasthani pancake which is distributed to thousands of people during the various festivals in Triveni, a small village about 80 miles from Jaipur. There is a very famous ashram from the Ramanuja sampradaya. There is also a temple of Their Lordships Sri Sri Sita Rama to whom the people are very much devoted. Different temples in Jaipur also offer mitha poora as a regular sweet.

Preparation and cooking time: about 1 hour
Makes: 16 pieces

½ cup jaggery
2½ cups (600 ml) water
1 cup whole wheat flour
1 teaspoon fennel seeds
25 whole black peppers
ghee for frying

1. Boil the water and add the jaggery.
2. Stirring occasionally, cook over medium heat until the jaggery is completely dissolved. This will take 12-15 minutes. Set aside until it is a little cooled down.
3. Place the flour in a mixing bowl. Slowly add the warm jaggery syrup into the flour and mix it with a whisk. There should not be any lumps and the consistency should be like pancake batter. You can add extra warm water if required. Add the fennel seeds and whole black peppers into the batter. Let sit for 12-15 minutes.

4. Pre-heat a non-stick, flat griddle. When it reaches medium heat, spread 2-3 teaspoons of ghee into the pan with a wooden spatula. Put 1/5 cup of batter onto the middle of the griddle. Let the batter sit for 4-5 seconds, then place a round spoon in the center of the batter and pressing lightly, spread the batter outward in a continuous, round motion to make a 2½" diameter mitha poora.

5. After 2-3 minutes, drizzle 1 teaspoon of ghee around the edge of the pancake. Cook the pancake for 3-4 minutes on the first side then carefully turn the mitha poora over with a wooden spatula. Drizzle ¾ teaspoon of ghee over its surface and ¾ teaspoon ghee around the edge of the pancake. Cook 3-4 minutes. You can stack these like regular pancakes.

6. Offer the hot mitha poora to Lord Krishna.

Note: Whole wheat flour should be used in this recipe instead of chapati flour because chapatti flour is too smooth for this recipe.

Malpoora

There is a very famous festival in India named Raksha Bandhan which happens to fall on Lord Balarama's appearance day. Lord Balarama is Lord Krishna's older brother. On this day, the women tie a thread on their brothers' wrists, and the brothers promise to protect their sisters. Some women also offer a thread to Lord Balarama and they receive everlasting protection from Him. This malpoora is offered with kheer (sweet rice) to the Deities during this festival.

Cooking and preparation time: about 30 minutes
Makes: 10 pieces

2 cups sugar
1½ cups (360 ml) water
½ tablespoon rose water
1 cup all-purpose flour
½ teaspoon cardamom powder
¼ teaspoon saffron
½ teaspoon baking powder
11/3 cups (320 ml) (or as required) whole milk
2 tablespoons chopped pistachios
ghee for deep frying

1. Boil the sugar and water in a 3-quart saucepan over medium heat until the sugar dissolves. Raise the heat to high and boil for 3-5 minutes more. Remove the pan from the heat and set it aside. Add the rose water.

2. Mix the flour, cardamom powder, saffron and baking powder in a bowl. Slowly add the milk and beat with a whisk until the mixture becomes very smooth. The consistency should be like pancake batter.

3. Heat ghee in a 2½" (6.5 cm) deep frying pan until it reaches 250°F (121°C). Pour 1/3 cup batter and with a round spoon, spread the batter in a circle to make a 4" diameter malpoora. Place as many circles of batter into the ghee as you can without crowding them. Cook on one side until they becomes light brown. This will take about 5 minutes. Maintain the temperature between 250°F (121°C) to 300°F (148°C) while you are frying; do not allow the temperature to increase.

4. Turn the malpoora over with a wooden spatula. Cook the other side for about 3 minutes so it becomes light brown. Carefully remove the malpoora with a slotted spoon and place into the syrup. Let soak for about 2-3 minutes, then remove and decorate with the chopped pistachios.

5. Offer hot malpoora to Lord Krishna.

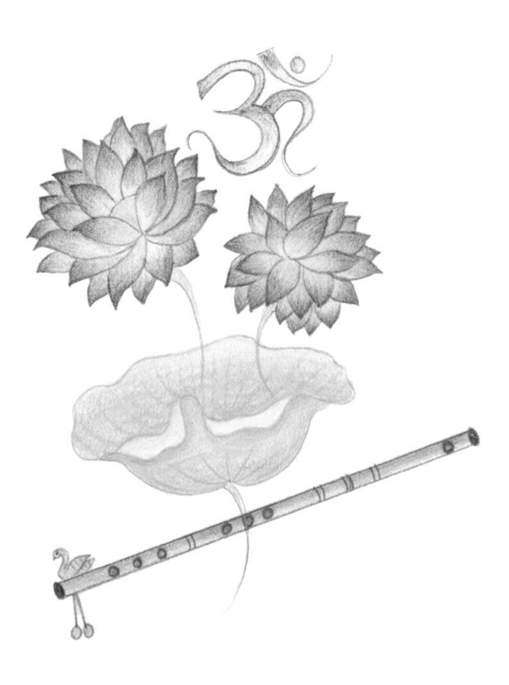

Partty Supta

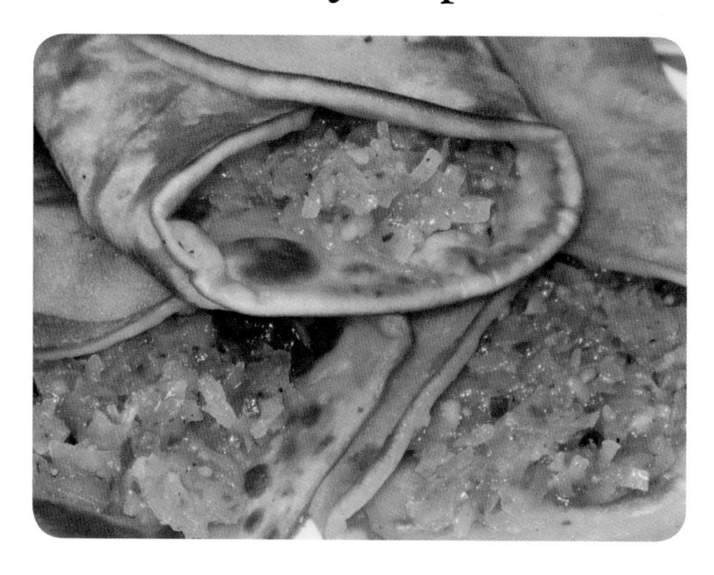

His Divine Grace Srila Prabhupada's Bengali disciple, His Grace Bankim Roy, shared this recipe with me which his grandmother used to make during his childhood. Though no longer common in Bengal, it is still a wonderful sweet to make for Lord Krishna.

Preparation and cooking time: about 35 minutes
Makes: 5 pieces

1 tablespoon ghee or unsalted butter
1½ cups dried, grated coconut
2 tablespoons chopped dates
2 tablespoons chopped pistachios or almonds
1 tablespoon raisins
1 teaspoon cardamom powder
½ cup sugar
1/3 cup (80 ml) whole milk
1½ cups (360ml) (or as required) whole milk
1 cup all-purpose flour
¾ cup powdered sugar
½ teaspoon baking powder
ghee for frying

1. Heat the one tablespoon of ghee or unsalted butter in a 3-quart saucepan. Add the dried, grated coconut and stirring constantly, cook over medium heat for about 2 minutes. Add the chopped dates, nut, raisins and ½ teaspoon cardamom powder. Stirring constantly, cook for about 1 minute more. Add the sugar and 1/3 cup of milk. Cook until the mixture becomes sticky (about 2 minutes). Place the pan aside to cool down and then divide the mixture into 5 portions.

2. Place the flour, baking powder, ½ teaspoon cardamom powder and powdered sugar in a bowl. With a whisk, beat in enough milk to make a smooth batter.

3. Pre-heat a non-stick, flat griddle for 3-4 minutes. When it reaches medium heat, spread 2-3 teaspoons of ghee onto the griddle with a wooden spatula. Pour ½ cup of the batter in the middle. Let the batter sit for 4-5 seconds, then place a round spoon into the center of the batter and pressing lightly, spread the batter outward in a continuous, circular motion and make a 5½" diameter partty supta. After 2-3 minutes, drizzle 1 teaspoon around the edge of the pancake. Cook for 3-4 minutes on the first side then with a wooden spatula, carefully turn the pancake over. Drizzle ¾ teaspoon ghee over the surface and ¾ teaspoon around the edge of the pancake. Cook 3-4 minutes.

4. Take one portion of the coconut mixture and place it in the middle of the pancake. Fold both edges to the center like a masala dosa.

5. Offer to Lord Krishna.

Coconut Laddu

Lord Krishna is also known as 'Laddu Gopal' because He is very fond of laddu. Once I thought I should try a different laddu for Gopal and after making them like this, I saw that the New Goloka devotees liked them very much.

Preparation and cooking time: about 1 hour 10 minutes
Makes: 24 pieces

3 cups grated, dried coconut
4 cups (960 ml) milk
1¾ cups sugar
½ cup grated, dried coconut for garnish

1. Grind 3 cups of coconut and about 2½ cups of milk in the blender until it becomes a smooth paste. Transfer the mixture to a 3-quart saucepan.
2. Add the remaining milk and stirring occasionally, bring to a boil. Reduce the heat to medium and stirring constantly, cook for 20-25 minutes so the mixture thickens.
3. Add the sugar and cook for about 12-15 minutes more so the mixture thickens again.
4. Allow the mixture to cool and roll into medium-sized balls, then roll into the remaining coconut.
5. Offer to Lord Krishna.

Date and Nut Laddu

I want to share a nice experience I had with this sweet. One devotee's mother, who was not directly connected with Krishna consciousness, was not able to take any sugar in the final stage of her life. However, she really liked this sweet and ate it. Fortunately she received Krishna's mercy through this prasad.

Preparation and cooking time: about 20 minutes
Makes: 12 pieces

1/3 cup almonds
1/3 cup pistachios
1/3 cup cashews
1½ cups pitted dates
¼ cup ghee or unsalted butter
½ cup grated, dried coconut

1. Grind all the nuts together in a food processor, place them in a bowl, then grind the dates adding a little water if necessary.
2. Melt the ghee or unsalted butter in a 3-quart saucepan and add the nuts. Stirring constantly, cook over medium heat for 4-5 minutes or until they become light brown. Turn off the heat, add the ground dates and mix well.
3. Roll the mixture into medium-sized balls and then roll into the coconut.
4. Offer to Lord Krishna.

Gond Ke Laddu

This is a traditional Rajasthani laddu which is cooked in the wintertime and is considered good for one's health. This is also eaten by Rajasthani mothers for the first forty days after they give birth to a child.

Cooking and preparation time: about 1 hour 15 minutes
Makes: 32 laddus

½ cup gond (edible gum available at Indian grocery stores)
2½ cups ghee or unsalted butter
4 cups whole wheat flour (chapati flour is best)
1 cup ground almonds
1 cup dried, grated coconut
2½ cups powdered sugar
ghee for deep frying

Grind the gond in a food processor for a few seconds or until it breaks into small pieces, Then fry it in the ghee in a 2½" (6.5 cm) deep frying pan over 300°F (148°C) temperature. It will puff and become about three times larger than it was originally. It will take about 2-3 minutes. Drain the gond and set aside.

2. Place the ghee or unsalted butter in a 6-quart stockpot and add the flour. Stirring constantly, cook over medium heat for about 20 minutes or until it changes color.

3. Transfer to a mixing bowl and add the grated coconut, ground almonds and fried gond. Mix well. Cool the mixture down and add the powdered sugar.

4. Mix well and roll into medium-sized balls.

5. Offer to Lord Krishna.

Note: There is another way to make this sweet. You can grind the edible gum (gond) in a food processor to make a fine powder. After cooking the chapati flour in ghee for 10 minutes, you add the ground gond and cook it with the flour.

Churma Laddu

Churma is another traditional Rajasthani sweet which is generally offered with dal (Indian lentil soup). It is not easily available in sweet shops but is distributed during big festivals to thousands of people in Jaipur. Usually only the churma mixture is offered and distributed in Jaipur, but I am adding extra ghee to make this laddu.

Preparation and cooking time: about 1½ hours
Makes: 28 pieces

3 cups whole wheat flour
1 cup semolina
2 cups melted ghee or unsalted butter
1¼ cups (300 ml) (or as required) warm milk
¾ teaspoon cardamom powder
3 tablespoons chopped pistachios
3 tablespoons chopped almonds
3 tablespoons chopped cashews
2 cups powdered sugar
ghee for deep frying

1. Combine the flour, semolina and ½ cup melted ghee or butter in a mixing bowl. Mix well and then add enough warm milk to make dough which is not too soft and not too firm. Roll 28-30 medium-sized balls.

2. Heat the ghee in a 6-quart stockpot until the temperature reaches 250°F (121°C). Drop the balls into the ghee without crowding them. Move them a few times with a wooden spatula and fry them until they turn golden brown. Repeat the same process until all the balls are fried, maintaining a temperature of 250°F (121°C) to 300°F (148°C). This will take about 10 minutes.

3. Remove the balls with a slotted spoon and allow them to cool down. Break them into small pieces. If you feel the balls are not cooked inside properly, you can fry them again for 4-5 minutes.

4. In a food processor, grind the small pieces until they become granulated. Transfer to a mixing bowl and add the cardamom powder, chopped nuts and powdered sugar. Add the remaining 1½ cups melted ghee. Mix well and roll into medium-sized balls.

5. Offer to Lord Krishna.

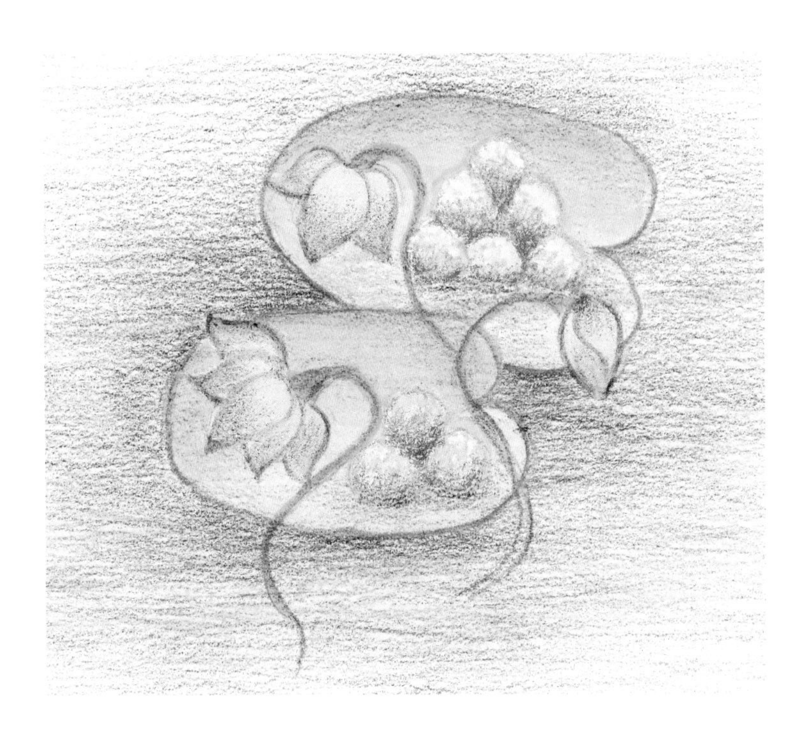

Besan Laddu

I have changed the regular besan laddu recipe by adding semolina. This laddu is regularly offered to Sri Sri Radha Golokananda in New Goloka in Hillsborough, NC.

Preparation and cooking time: about 1 hour
Makes: 24 pieces

1¾ cups ghee or unsalted butter
1 cup semolina
3 cups chickpea flour
2 cups powdered sugar

1. Melt the ghee or butter in a 3-quart saucepan. Add the semolina and stirring constantly, cook for 5 minutes over medium heat. Add the chickpea flour and turn the heat to low. Cook for 15-20 minutes or until the chickpea flour deepens in color. Turn off the heat and stir 5 minutes more.
2. Transfer the mixture to a bowl and add the powdered sugar. Mix well. Let the mixture cool down or place it in the refrigerator to cool down faster. Roll into smooth, medium-sized balls.
3. Offer to Lord Krishna.

Note: To make very smooth and round laddus, I put them in the refrigerator after rolling them. Then, after a few minutes, I take them out and softly roll them again.

Bundi Laddu

Bundi laddu is offered on every offering every day to Sri Sri Radha Govinda Dev Ji in Jaipur. On Ekadasi, they are made with buckwheat flour. There was an article about Sri Sri Radha Govinda Dev Ji temple in the Back to Godhead magazine from May/June 1997 and it was mentioned that more than 10,000 laddus are made every day and many more on festival days.

Preparation and cooking time: about 1 hour
Makes: 20 pieces

1½ cups sugar
1¼ (300 ml) cups water
2 cups laddu besan (available at Indian grocery stores)
1¼ teaspoons crushed cardamom
½ teaspoon saffron
3 tablespoons char magaz (cantaloupe seeds – optional)
ghee for deep frying

1. Boil the sugar and water in a 3-quart saucepan over medium heat and stir occasionally until the sugar dissolves. Raise the heat and boil the syrup for 8-10 minutes more. Set the pan aside and add the cardamom and saffron.

2. Place the besan flour in a mixing bowl. Add enough water, and using a whisk make a smooth batter. The batter should not be too thick or too thin.

3. Heat the ghee in a 6-quart stockpot over a high heat until it reaches 325°F (162°C). Hold a perforated spoon or colander over the hot ghee and pour approximately ½ cup batter into it. Push the batter through into the hot ghee with the back of a measuring cup or round spoon so chickpea flour pearls or droplets can fall into the hot ghee.

4. Fry for 2-3 minutes. The bundi (chickpea flour pearls or droplets) should turn a light golden brown; take care to ensure that they are not too crisp.

5. Remove the bundi from the ghee with a deep slotted spoon and transfer into the sugar syrup. Repeat this process until all the batter is made into bundis.

5. With a wooden spoon, mix the bundi and sugar syrup well. Grind 2 cups of the bundi mixture in the food processor for about 20 seconds; this will allow easy and smooth rolling. Mix the ground bundi mixture with the remaining bundi. Add the char magaz. Moisten your hands and roll the mixture into medium-sized balls.

7. Offer to Lord Krishna.

Til Ke Laddu

Each year in Rajasthan on January 14, there is the famous Makar Sankranti festival as well as the kite festival when everyone flies their kites high into the sky. At this time, it is tradition for everyone to give donations of this sweet to the temples and brahmanas.

Preparation and cooking time: about 45 minutes
Makes: 20 pieces

1 cup peanuts without skins
2 cups til (sesame seeds)
1½ cups jaggery
1 cup ghee or unsalted butter

1. Grind the peanuts in a food processor for about 1-2 minutes. Set aside. Grind 1 cup of the sesame seeds in a blender for 1-2 minutes. Set aside.

2. Melt 2 tablespoons of ghee or unsalted butter in a 3-quart saucepan. First add the ground peanuts and stirring constantly, cook over medium heat for 3-4 minutes. Add the whole sesame seeds, cook for 3-4 minutes, and then add the ground sesame seeds. Cook for 5-7 minutes more.

3. Add the jaggery and cook over low heat until it is melted and mixed well with the sesame seed and peanut mixture. This will take 7-8 minutes.

4. Transfer this to a mixing bowl and add the remaining melted ghee or unsalted butter. Mix well. Let it cool down for 8-10 minutes.

5. When the mixture is warm, with moist hands roll into medium-sized balls.

6. Offer to Lord Krishna.

Note: If the mixture is too dry to roll into balls, add more melted ghee or unsalted butter. There are also different colors of sesame seeds; I am using white sesame seeds for this sweet.

Basundi

This is a famous Gujarati milk sweet. Nuts are used instead of rice which make this preparation very opulent and is good for Ekadasi.

Preparation and cooking time: about 30 minutes
Serves: 4 persons

4 cups (960 ml or 1 liter) milk
1/3 cup sugar
¼ teaspoon cardamom powder
1 tablespoons chopped cashews
1 tablespoons chopped pistachios

1. Pour the milk into a thick-bottomed 3-quart saucepan and over high heat, bring to a boil. Stir so the milk doesn't stick to the pot. Reduce the heat to medium and stir frequently.
2. Simmer the milk for about 15-20 minutes so it cooks down to 2/3 its original quantity. Add the sugar and cook 5 minutes more
3. Add the cardamom powder and chopped nuts. Allow the mixture to cool.
4. Offer to Lord Krishna chilled.

Paneer Ki Kheer

This kheer tastes like rasamalai and is a wonderful preparation to offer Lord Krishna on Janmastami. My special thanks to my sister, Sunita Agarwal, for encouraging me to try this recipe.

Preparation and cooking time: about 1 hour
Serves: 6 persons

5 oz. (142 g or ¾ cup) paneer
8 cups (1920 ml or 2 liters) whole milk
½ tablespoon rose water
2 tablespoons chopped pistachios
½ teaspoon cardamom powder
¼ teaspoon saffron
1 cup sugar
1 cup (240 ml) water

1. Rinse paneer thoroughly (in a cheese cloth) under cold water. This will remove the sour taste.
2. Stirring occasionally, bring the milk to a boil in a 6-quart stockpot. Reduce the heat to medium and simmer for about 30 minutes so it cooks down to 2/3 its original quantity. Add the chopped pistachios, cardamom powder and saffron. Transfer to a mixing bowl. Allow it to cool down.
3. Combine the sugar and water in a 3-quart saucepan. Bring to a boil over medium heat and stirring occasionally, cook it for 10 minutes. Add the paneer to the sugar water and cook for 2 minutes. Pour the paneer and sugar mixture into the cooled kheer and mix the rose water in.
4. Offer to Lord Krishna.

Mango Rabri

Mango kulfi is very famous in Jaipur. I cooked mango rabri for the Deities. Mango rabri becomes kulfi by putting it in the freezer for a few hours.

Preparation and cooking time: about 40 minutes
Serves: 4 persons

4 cups (960 ml or 1 liter) whole milk
½ cup sugar
½ cup mango puree

1. Pour the milk into a 3-quart saucepan and, stirring occasionally, bring to a boil over high heat.

2. Reduce the heat to medium and stir occasionally while the milk gently boils. As the milk thickens, scrape it from the sides of the pan with a wooden spatula. Simmer the milk until the volume is one-third its original quantity. This will take 20-25 minutes. Add the sugar and cook down for 5-7 minutes more.

4. Place the rabri in the refrigerator to cool down; then add the mango puree. Mix well.

5. Offer chilled or frozen to Lord Krishna.

Fruits and Nuts Kheer

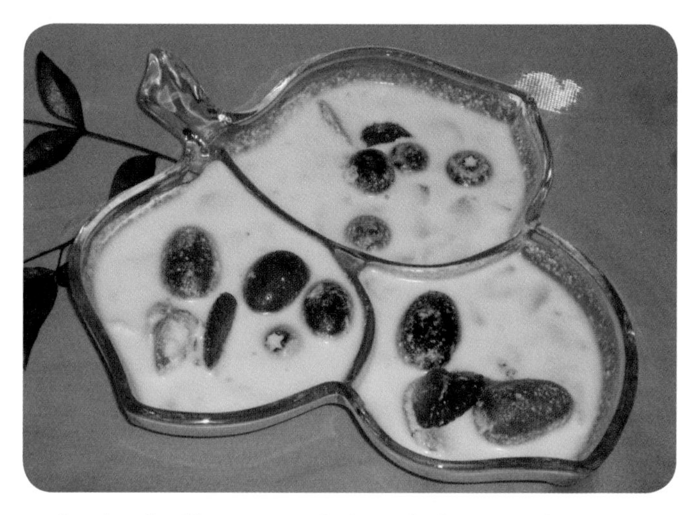

I remember that this kheer was cooked on Ekadasi at my home in Jaipur. It gives energy and although it does not have much sugar and is cooked without butter, it is still very filling.

Preparation and cooking time: about 40 minutes
Serves: 4 persons

4 cups (960 ml or 1 liter) whole milk
1 tablespoon chopped pistachios
1 tablespoon chopped almonds
1 tablespoon chopped cashews
3 tablespoons sugar
1 cup cut mixed fruits like banana, pomegranate, grapes, blueberry, apple

1. Boil the milk over high heat in a 6-quart stockpot. Reduce the heat to medium and stirring occasionally, simmer the milk for 20 minutes or until it cooks down to ¾ its original quantity. Add the nuts and sugar and cook for 5 minutes more.
2. Place the mixture in the refrigerator and allow it to cool. Mix the fruits into the cooled kheer.
3. Offer to Lord Krishna chilled.

Note: It is very important that the milk be cooled down before you add the fruits, otherwise the milk will curdle.

Ekadasi Kheer

This kheer is made with samo which is good for Ekadasi. I received this preparation in Vrindavan which brought back fond memories of the kheer I had during my childhood in Jaipur.

Preparation and cooking time: about 40 minutes
Serves: 4 persons

4 cups (960 ml or 1 liter) whole milk
¼ cup samo (available at Indian grocery stores)
½ cup sugar
1 tablespoon charoli seeds (optional)

1. Boil the milk in a 6-quart stockpot over high heat. Reduce the heat to medium and cook for 8-10 minutes.
2. Wash the samo thoroughly and add to the boiling milk. Stir occasionally until the samo is completely cooked and the kheer is ¾'s its original quantity. This will take about 20 minutes.
3. Add the sugar and charoli. Cook for 7-8 minutes more.
4. Offer to Lord Krishna chilled or at room temperature.

Doodh Poha

'Sarad Purnim,' the first day of the month of Kartik, is a very important day on the Vedic calendar as Lord Krishna performed His special pastime with His gopi friends. There is a tradition in Rajastan that kheer (sweet rice) is cooked and on this evening, the pot of kheer is covered with a thin cloth and is then put on the roof. It is believed that the moon showers nectar on this night. The next morning, the kheer is offered to the Deities and then distributed. The same tradition is followed in Gujarat, India but instead of kheer, doodh poha is cooked and is kept only for few hours on the roof that night.

Cooking and preparation time: about 35 minutes
Serves: 4 persons

4 cups (960 ml or 1 liter) milk
½ cup thick poha (flat rice) available at Indian grocery stores
¼ cup sugar
1 tablespoon chopped almonds
1 tablespoon chopped pistachios
¼ teaspoon cardamom powder

1. Boil the milk in a heavy-bottomed, 3-quart saucepan over high heat. Reduce the heat to medium and stir occasionally. Cook the milk for 10-12 minutes or until 2/3 of the original quantity remains. Be careful the milk does not stick to the bottom of the pan.

2. Wash the thick poha (flat rice) under running water and add to the boiling milk. Cook for 12-15 minutes more or until the flat rice becomes soft. Stir occasionally.

3. Add the sugar, cardamom powder and chopped nuts and cook 5 minutes more.

4. Offer to Lord Krishna chilled or at room temperature.

Kheer

Once while visiting the Sri Sri Radha Damodar Temple in Vrindavan with my husband, the pujari gave us kheer maha prasadam. I found the taste was very different from what I had ever had, and it was so wonderful! He told us that date jaggery is used instead of regular sugar to sweeten this kheer. It is definitely worthwhile to make this kheer for Lord Krishna. If you do not have date jaggery, then you can use regular jaggery.

Preparation and cooking time: about 40 minutes
Serves: 3 to 4 persons

2 tablespoons basmati rice
4 cups (960 ml or 1 liter) whole milk
¼ cup date jaggery
¼ teaspoon cardamom powder
1 tablespoon chopped almonds

1. Soak the rice in water for 10-12 minutes.
2. Boil the milk in a heavy-bottomed, 3-quart saucepan over high heat. Reduce the heat to medium and cook for 10 minutes. Stir frequently so the milk does not stick to the pan.
3. Wash the rice under running water until the water becomes clear and then add the rice to the boiling milk. Stirring frequently, cook the rice until it is soft and the milk is about ½ the original quantity. It will take 18-20 minutes. Add the cardamom powder and chopped almonds. Transfer kheer in a mixing bowl and leave aside for 20-22 minutes.
4. While the kheer is warm, add the jaggery and mix well.
5. Offer to Lord Krishna chilled or at room temperature.

Note: If the kheer is too hot when you add the jaggery, the milk will curdle.

Pistachio and Pineapple Phirni

It is always very pleasing to try and cook different milk sweets for Lord Krishna Who is protector of cows and Who is very fond of milk sweets.

Preparation and cooking time: about 1 hour
Serves: 4 persons

1/3 cup basmati rice
½ cup pistachios
1½ cups (360 ml) boiling water
4 cups (960 ml or 1 liter) whole milk
1 cup sugar
1 cup pineapple cut into small pieces

1. Wash the rice and pistachios thoroughly under running water. Soak in boiling hot water for 20-25 minutes.
2. Place the rice, pistachios, and water together into a blender and blend them until the mixture becomes a smooth puree.
3. Place the milk in a 3-quart, non-stick pan. Stirring occasionally, boil over medium heat.
4. With your left hand, slowly pour the puree into the milk while stirring constantly with your right hand. This will prevent lumps. Follow this process until the whole puree is poured into the milk. Cook for 12-15 minutes on medium heat, stirring constantly.
5. Add the sugar and bring everything to a boil. Cook over medium heat for 4-5 minutes or until it becomes thick. Then transfer into a mixing bowl and refrigerate for a few hours. Add the cut pineapple to the chilled phirni.
6. Offer to Lord Krishna.

Shrikhand

Once, when I was visiting a Gujarati family, I received the thickest, creamiest shrikhand I have ever had! The mataji of the house shared her technique with me and I shall now share it with you.

Preparation time: about 20 minutes
Yogurt draining time: 6-8 hours
Serves: 4 to 6 persons

4 cups (960 ml or 1 liter) whole milk yogurt
½ cup sugar
cheesecloth

1. Place the yogurt in 2 layers of cheesecloth and hang it in the refrigerator for 6-8 hours over a bowl to catch the dripping whey. After all the whey has dripped out, take a pile of newspapers and put a paper towel on it. While the yogurt is still in the cheesecloth, place it on top of the paper towel. Cover it with another paper towel and another layer of newspaper. Place a heavy weight on top. After 5-7 minutes, the newspaper will have absorbed any extra moisture. If you want thicker yogurt, then repeat this procedure.
2. Scrape the yogurt from the cloth with a spoon and transfer it into a mixing bowl. Add the sugar and beat with a whisk until the shrikhand becomes light and fluffy.
3. Offer to Lord Krishna chilled or at room temperature.

Note: I like to add fresh-cut fruits like strawberries, blueberries, pineapple, mango or peaches to the shrikhand to offer to Sri Sri Radha Golokananda on Janmastami.

Rasgoola

His Divine Grace Srila Prabhupada was from Bengal and always enjoyed this traditional Bengali sweet, rasgoola. Because of this, I always had a desire to make squeaky rasgoolas for him. (Rasgoolas are considered successfully made when they squeak.) It is therefore my great fortune that every year I get the chance to make rasgoolas to offer to him on his appearance day. My special thanks to mother Uttara for teaching me to make rasgoolas.

Preparation and cooking time: about 1¼ hours
Makes: 16 pieces

7 cups (1680 ml) water
4 cups sugar
10 oz. (285 g or 1½ cups) paneer
½ tablespoon rose water

1. Combine 2 cups water and 2 cups sugar in a 3-quart saucepan and stirring occasionally, bring to a boil over medium heat until the sugar dissolves. Increase the heat to high and boil for about 5 minutes more. Transfer to a mixing bowl and add the rose water. Set this aside and allow the sugar syrup to cool.

2. Press the paneer under a heavy weight until the liquid is drained and the paneer becomes firm. It will take about 30-40 minutes. Break the paneer into small pieces and blend in the food processor until the paneer becomes smooth. This will take about 2 minutes. Roll the paneer into medium-sized but not very smooth balls. Do not press the balls too much while rolling them. Set them aside.

3. Boil the remaining 2 cups sugar and 5 cups water in a 6-quart stockpot. Drop the balls one-by-one into the boiling sugar syrup. Cover the pan and boil over high heat for about 15-18 minutes. The balls will swell to double or triple in size. Uncover the pan and sprinkle cold water over the boiling rasgoolas; this helps to make them squeaky. Cover them again and repeat this process every 2-3 minutes for 15 minutes.

4. Take the rasgoolas carefully from the hot sugar syrup and transfer them into the cooled syrup. Let them soak in the syrup for at least 4 hours.

5. Offer to Lord Krishna.

Raj Bhoga

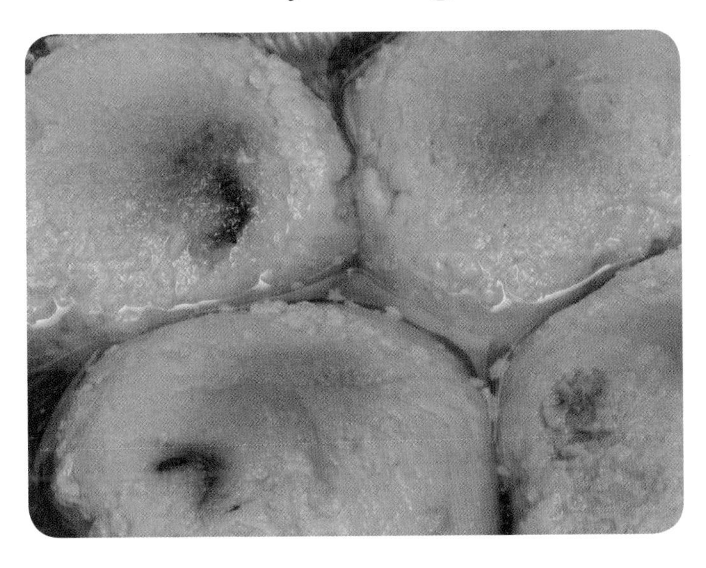

Some people in Jaipur believe that raj bhoga is one of Lord Rama's favorite sweets. Whether this statement is bonafide or not, we don't know, but this sweet is definitely wonderful to offer to the Supreme Personality of Godhead, Lord Krishna or Lord Rama.

Preparation and cooking time: about 1¼ hours
Makes: 12 pieces

7 cups (1680 ml) water
4 cups sugar
½ tablespoon rose water
10 oz. (285 g or 1½ cups) paneer
1½ tablespoons chopped pistachios
1 teaspoon crushed cardamom
½ teaspoon saffron
yellow food coloring

1. Combine 2 cups of water and 2 cups of sugar in a 3-quart saucepan over medium heat. Stirring occasionally, bring to a boil until the sugar dissolves. Increase the heat to high and boil for about 5 minutes more. Transfer to a mixing bowl.
2. Add the rose water and set it aside to let the sugar syrup cool.

3. Press the paneer under a heavy weight until the liquid drains and it is firm. It will take 30-40 minutes. Break the paneer into small pieces and place in a food processor. Add 18-20 drops of yellow food coloring and blend until the paneer becomes smooth. This will take about 2 minutes.

4. Mix the chopped pistachios, cardamom and saffron in a bowl.

5. Divide the paneer into 12 portions and then roll them into balls. Flatten them between your palms and place ½ teaspoon of pistachio mixture in the middle. Fold the edge over the nuts so it is closed, then gently roll them into balls again. The balls should not be very smooth. Set them aside.

6. Boil the remaining sugar and water (2 cups sugar and 5 cups water) in a 6-quart stockpot. Add about 30 drops of yellow food coloring to the boiling water. Drop the balls one-by-one into the boiling sugar syrup. Cover the pan. Boil the balls over high heat for 20-22 minutes. The balls will double or triple in size.

7. Carefully take the raj bhoga out from the hot sugar syrup and soak them in the cooled syrup for at least 4 hours.

8. Offer to Lord Krishna.

Pistachios Rasmalai

Usually rasmalai is cooked without adding any food coloring, but I like to use different flavors and colors when I make this on Janmastami for Sri Sri Radha Golokananda. I use red coloring and rose water to make rose rasmalai and yellow coloring and saffron to make saffron rasmalai.

Preparation and cooking time: about 1¼ hours
Makes: 16 pieces

4 cups (960 ml or 1 liter) whole milk
2½ cups sugar
½ teaspoon cardamom powder
½ tablespoon rose water
1½ tablespoons chopped pistachios
Green food coloring
10 oz. (285 g or 1½ cups) paneer
5 cups (1200 ml) water

1. Stirring occasionally, boil the milk in a 3-quart saucepan over medium heat for about 20-25 minutes. Add ½ cup sugar and the cardamom powder. Boil for 3-5 minutes more then transfer to a mixing bowl. Add the rose water, chopped pistachios and 8-10 drops of green food coloring. Set aside to cool down.

2. Press the paneer under a heavy weight until the liquid drains and the paneer becomes firm. This will take 30-40 minutes. Break the paneer into small pieces and place in a food processor. Add 18-20 drops of green food coloring and blend until the paneer becomes smooth. This will take about 2 minutes. Divide the paneer into 16 portions and roll them into balls. Flatten the balls between your palms and set aside.

3. Boil the remaining 2 cups of sugar with the water in a 6-quart stockpot and add about 25 drops of the green food coloring. One-by-one, drop the rasmalai into the boiling sugar syrup. Cover the pan. Boil over high heat for 22-25 minutes. The balls will double or triple in size.

4. Remove the rasmalai carefully from the hot sugar syrup and place them into the cooled, sweetened milk. Allow them to soak for at least 4 hours.

5. Offer to Lord Krishna.

Kalakand

Kalakand is a very famous milk sweet made in Jaipur. I remember, as kids, we used to have cake made with kalakand on our birthday.

Preparation and cooking time: about 40 minutes
Makes: 16 pieces

10 oz. (285 g or 1½ cups) paneer
1 cup (240 ml) whole milk
½ cup sugar
¼ teaspoon cardamom powder

1. Knead the paneer with your hands so the texture is soft but not very smooth.
2. Boil the milk in a 3-quart saucepan over medium heat and add the paneer. Stirring constantly, cook over medium heat until the liquid evaporates and the mixture becomes thick. This will take 7-8 minutes. Add the sugar and cardamom powder and keep stirring until the excess liquid evaporates. This will take 8-10 minutes more.
3. Spread the kalakand in a greased 8" x 8" x 2" baking tray and allow it to cool down. Cut into squares.
4. Offer to Lord Krishna.

Steamed Sandesh

One time while I was visiting my family in Jaipur, I got the chance to take a cooking class from a woman named Reena Jain who shared different kinds of sandesh recipes with me. I really like this particular recipe.

Preparation and cooking time: about 40 minutes
Makes: 8 pieces

10 oz. (285 g or 1½ cups) paneer
½ cup sugar
1½ tablespoons chopped pistachios
1/3 teaspoon saffron
½ tablespoon rose water

1. Place the paneer in a mixing bowl. Knead it with your hand until it becomes soft but not too smooth. Add the sugar and mix well with your hands.

2. Place a few inches of water in a 6-quart stockpot. With ghee or unsalted butter, grease a 2" deep cake pan that will fit comfortably inside the stockpot.

3. With your hand, press the paneer and sugar mixture into the cake pan. Decorate the paneer with the chopped pistachios and saffron.

4. Set a bowl or metal measuring cup upside-down inside the saucepan; it should sit above water level and below the top of the pan. Boil the water

over high heat and set the cake pan on top of the bowl or measuring cup. Cover the saucepan with a lid.

5. Turn the heat to medium and steam the sandesh for 10-12 minutes. Remove the cake pan and allow it to cool and set for a few hours.

6. Sprinkle rose water on top of the sandesh and cut into squares.

7. Offer to Lord Krishna.

Gur (Jaggery) Ke Sandesh

This is very famous sandesh from Bengal, India and is also known as 'manda'. It is cooked when fresh jaggery is made from dates. Date jaggery is available in Navadvip dham, Bengal. If you do not have date jaggery, you can use regular jaggery.

Preparation and cooking time: about 1 hour
Makes: 8 pieces

¾ cup jaggery
10 oz. (285 g or 1½ cups) paneer

1. To soften the jaggery, bake it in the oven for 8-10 minutes at 350 degree. Crush it by using a pastry roller or rolling pin.
2. Mix the paneer and jaggery well by using the palm of your hand. It will take 15-20 minutes to make a smooth mixture.
3. Transfer the mixture into a 3-quart saucepan and stirring constantly, cook over low heat for 10-12 minutes.
4. Allow the mixture to cool and divide into 8 portions. Roll them into your desired shape.
5. Offer to Lord Krishna.

Makhan Mishri Pera

It was a great fortune for my husband, Gopal Prabhu, and me to stay in Vrindavan for several months. While there, I noticed that almost all of the sweet shops sold small-sized, brown pera; I thought these must be Lord Krishna's favorite sweets! As Krishna is also known as Makhan Chor (the butter thief who likes to steal makhan or butter). Makhan (butter) mixed with mishri (sugar candy) is another of Lord Krishna's favorite sweets, I tried to combine both of them for His pleasure, the One Who is the source of all pleasures.

Preparation and cooking time: about 50 minutes
Makes: 8 pieces

4 cups (960 ml or 1 liter) whole milk
¼ cup dark brown sugar
2 tablespoons ground sugar candy
1 tablespoon unsalted, soft butter

1. Pour the milk into a heavy-bottomed, 3-quart saucepan. Bring the milk to a full, foaming boil over high heat. Turn the heat to medium making sure the milk continues to boil. Stir frequently with a wooden spatula to prevent the milk from sticking to the bottom of the pan. Boil for 15-17 minutes.

2. Turn the heat down to low. Stir constantly until the mixture becomes thick and sticky and pulls away from the sides of the pan. This will take 18-20 minutes. Add the sugar and cook for 5-7 minutes or until it thickens again. Transfer this into a mixing bowl and allow it to cool.

3. Mix the butter and sugar candy in a small bowl. Divide the pera mixture into 8 portions. Roll into smooth balls and then press them between your palms to flatten them.

4. Fill each patty with ¼ teaspoon of the butter and sugar candy mixture. Again roll into balls and press them between your palms to flatten them.

5. Offer to Lord Krishna.

Cashew Pera

Cooked down milk pera is a very famous sweet of Vrindavana dham. I tried to cook a different type of pera for Lord Krishna. This sweet is quite elegant.

Preparation and cooking time: about 30 minutes
Makes: 16 pieces

2 cups cashew pieces
1 cup sugar

1. Soak the cashews in water for 3-4 hours. Strain the water and grind the cashews to a fine paste in a food processor. Add a little water if necessary. Transfer this to a 3- quart saucepan.
2. Add the sugar and mix well using a whisk. Stirring constantly, cook the mixture over low heat for about 15-20 minutes.
3. Cool down the mixture and divide it into 16 pieces. Roll each portion into a smooth ball and then press it into a decorative mold. (You can also make round or flat pieces.)
4. Set the sweets either in a greased pan or on waxed paper.
5. Offer to Lord Krishna.

Gulab Jamun

For those who may not know, in the early days of the movement, Srila Prabhupada would keep a jar of gulab jamuns (known as ISKCON bullets) on his desk for distribution. I always wanted an easy and exact gulab jamun recipe and am therefore very thankful to Yadurani mataji for having shared this recipe with me. I also feel very encouraged because Apurva prabhu, a highly-accomplished cook, called me to get this recipe, which he now uses for his prasadam distribution program.

Preparation and cooking time: about 1 hour 15 minutes
Makes: 28 pieces

3 cups sugar
4 cups (460 ml) water
½ tablespoon rose water
2 cups instant, non-fat dry milk powder
½ cup white flour
1 teaspoon crushed cardamom
½ teaspoon saffron
1/3 cup melted ghee
½ teaspoon baking powder
¾ cup (180 ml) (or as required) warm milk
ghee for deep frying

1. Combine the sugar and water in a 3-quart saucepan. Stirring occasionally, boil over medium heat until the sugar dissolves. Raise the heat to high and boil for 5 more minutes. Remove the pan from the heat and set it aside, then add the rose water.

2. Combine the milk powder, white flour, baking powder, crushed cardamom and saffron in a bowl. Add the melted ghee and mix it together with your hands, then add enough warm milk to make soft dough. Divide the dough into 28 portions. Roll each portion between your palms into a smooth ball and place them on a greased plate.

3. Heat the ghee in a 6-quart stockpot until the temperature reaches to 215°F (101°C). Slip the balls into the ghee without crowding them as they will double in size while frying. They will sink to the bottom of the ghee in the beginning. Do not move them with a spoon, but gently shake the pan so the balls do not stick to the bottom and burn. After 5-7 minutes, the balls will rise to the surface. Now constantly and gently turn the balls around with a wooden spatula.

4. Cook the balls until they become golden brown. This will take about 12-15 minutes. Maintain the temperature of the ghee between 215°F (101°C) and 250°F (121°C).

5. Remove the balls from the ghee with a slotted spoon and soak them in the sugar syrup for at least 2-3 hours before offering. If the gulab jamuns collapse in the sugar syrup, remove them and dry them with a paper towel; then fry them for 3-4 minutes more.

6. Offer either hot or at room temperature to Lord Krishna.

Kala Jamun

Once I was visiting Shradhanjali devi dasi, a disciple of His Holiness Bhakti Caru Maharaja, who was cooking kala jamun for her home Deities, Sri Sri Krishna Balarama. It reminded me of Diwali in Jaipur when almost every sweet shop had this special sweet for sale. This is another sweet which is very much liked by the devotees in New Goloka. Many thanks to Shradhanjali for sharing this recipe.

Preparation and cooking time: about 1 hour 15 minutes
Makes: 20 pieces

3 cups sugar
2 cups (360 ml) water
2 cups instant, non-fat milk powder
1 cup unbleached white flour
1/3 teaspoon baking powder
1½ cups (360 ml) or as required whipping cream
1 cup dried, grated coconut
ghee for deep frying

1. Stirring occasionally, boil the sugar and water in a 3-quart saucepan over medium heat until the sugar dissolves. Raise the heat and boil 5-7 minutes more. Set aside.

2. Combine the milk powder, flour and baking powder in a mixing bowl. Add enough whipping cream to make soft dough. Divide the dough into 20 portions and roll each one into an oval shape.

3. Heat the ghee in a 6-quart stockpot until the temperature reaches 250°F (121°C). Slip as many kala jamun as you can fit into the pot without crowding them. They will sink at first, but do not move them with a spoon; gently shake the pan so the balls do not stick to the bottom and burn. After 5-7 minutes, the balls will rise to the surface. Now constantly and gently turn the balls around with a wooden spatula so they are evenly cooked. Maintaining a temperature of 250°F (121°C) to 300°F (148°C), fry the balls until they become almost black. This will take about 15-20 minutes. Remove the balls from the ghee and slip them into the sugar syrup.

4. Soak the kala jamuns in the syrup for 5-7 minutes then remove them one-by-one (so they don't dry out) and roll in the grated coconut.

5. Offer to Lord Krishna.

Jalebi

In Jaipur, the jalebis are offered to the Deities with hot milk. The milk is cooked down to thicken it, then saffron, cardamom and sugar are added; this is then offered with the hot jalebis. Although I tried several recipes, I finally found that this recipe, shared by my cousin's wife, Manjula Jeendgar, made the easiest and very crisp jalebis.

Preparation and cooking time: about 1 hour
Makes: 16 pieces

2 cups sugar
1 cup (240 ml) water
½ tablespoon rose water
1 cup unbleached white flour
2 tablespoons chickpea flour
1¼ cup or as required warm water
½ teaspoon saffron threads
½ teaspoon eno powder (available at Indian grocery stores)
ghee for deep frying
plastic squeeze bottle or quart zip lock bag

1. Combine the sugar and water in a 3-quart saucepan. Stirring occasionally, boil over moderate heat until the sugar dissolves. Raise the heat to high and boil for 4-5 minutes more. Remove the pan from the heat and add the rose water. Set aside.

2. Combine the white flour, chickpea flour and saffron in a bowl. Add enough warm water and whisk until the consistency is like pancake batter. Add the eno powder and whisk again. Pour the batter into a plastic squeeze bottle or quart size zip lock bag.

3. Heat the ghee in a 2½" (6.5 cm) deep frying pan until temperature reaches to 215°F (101°C).

4. To shape the jalebis, hold the bottle tightly in one hand and squeeze the batter into the hot ghee. If you are using a zip lock bag, cut one corner of the bag to make a small hole and squeeze the bag to get the batter out. Shape three connecting rings, double-figure eights, or a series of loops connected like a chain about 2x3 inches (5x7.5 cm) wide. Maintaining a temperature of 215°F (101°C) to 250°F (121°C), fry the jalebis for about 3-4 minutes or until they become golden brown. Carefully turn them over with a wooden spatula and fry them until crisp and golden brown (about 2 minutes). Using a slotted spoon, lift the jalebis carefully from the ghee and transfer them into the warm syrup. Soak them no more than 2-3 minutes (so they stay crisp) then remove them with a slotted spoon.

5. Offer to Lord Krishna.

Imarti

Another name for this sweet is kangan which is a very famous sweet in Jaipur. The color of this sweet is dark orange and its shape is similar to the jalebi. Sometimes people do not know about this sweet and think it is jalebi, but the taste and the ingredients are different. It also takes practice to make the proper shape.

Preparation and cooking time: about 1 hour 30 minutes
Makes: 16 pieces

1 cup urad dal without skin
red and yellow food coloring
3 cups sugar
1½ cups (360 ml) water
pastry bag or quart zip lock bag
ghee for deep frying

1. Soak the dal in water for 6-8 hours or overnight. Strain and rinse the dal under running water. Grind the dal in a food processor by adding a little water to make a smooth paste. Add enough red and yellow food coloring to make dark orange. Beat the mixture with either a whisk or an electric hand-mixer until it becomes fluffy and creamy. Set aside for 1-2 hours.

2. Boil the sugar and water in a 3 quart saucepan over medium heat until the sugar dissolves. Raise the heat to high and boil for 4-5 minutes more. Set aside.

3. Heat the ghee in a 2½" (6.5 cm) deep frying pan until the temperature reaches 250°F (121°C).

4. Take a pastry bag or cut a small corner of a quart-size zip lock bag and fill it half way with the mixture. To shape the imarti, squeeze the bag over the hot ghee and shape two 2" rings one inside the other. Then form small rings all around those rings. Fry 5-6 minutes on one side, then carefully turn them over with a wooden spatula. Fry 4-5 minutes more. The temperature can go up to 300°F (148°C) while frying. Follow this procedure until the mixture is finished.

5. Transfer the imarti into the sugar syrup. Soak for 4-6 minutes then carefully remove them.

6. Offer to Lord Krishna.

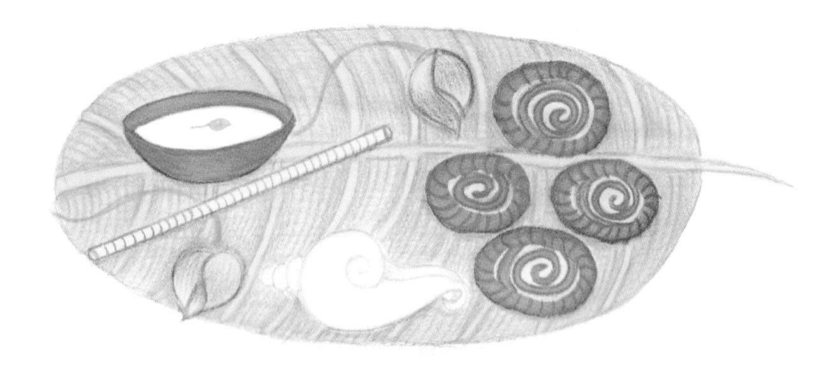

Gujiya

Gaura Purnima is a festival celebrating the appearance day of Sri Chaitanya Mahaprabhu. It is also the time of Holi, the festival of colors, when people throw colors on each other. At this time, the ladies in Jaipur cook gujiya at home and offer it to their Laddu Gopal Deity, the most common home deity in Rajasthan

Preparation and cooking time: about 1 hour 30 minutes
Makes: 20 pieces

2 cups white flour
¼ cup + 3 tablespoons ghee or unsalted butter
¾ cup (180 ml) or as required whole warm milk
2 cups sugar
1 cup (240 ml) water
¾ cup semolina
1/3 cup dried, grated coconut
1 tablespoon chopped pistachios
½ teaspoon cardamom powder
1 tablespoon charoli (available at Indian grocery store)
½ cup powdered sugar
ghee for deep frying

1. Mix the flour and ¼ cup melted ghee or unsalted butter in a mixing bowl. Add enough warm milk to make soft dough. Knead, cover and set aside.

2. Boil the sugar and water in a 3-quart saucepan over medium heat until the sugar dissolves. Raise the heat and boil for 4-5 minutes. Set aside.

3. Melt 3 tablespoons of ghee or unsalted butter in a 3-quart saucepan. Stirring constantly, add the semolina and cook until it changes color. This will take 10-12 minutes. Transfer this to a mixing bowl and add the dried, grated coconut, chopped pistachios, cardamom powder and charoli. Cool down and add the powdered sugar. Mix well.

4. Divide the dough into 20 portions. Roll each portion into a smooth ball then roll with roller into a 3-inch round. Place 1¼ teaspoon of the filling on half of a round, moisten the edge with water and fold over the side with the filling. Tightly press the edges together. Hold the gujiya in one hand and use the other hand to pinch and twist the sealed edge inwards like a samosa. Repeat this process to make all gujiyas. Seal carefully. If there are any holes, the filling will come out during the deep frying.

5. Heat the ghee in a 6-quart stockpot over moderate heat until the temperature reaches 250°F (121°C) without crowding them, carefully place the gujiya in the ghee. Maintaining a temperature of 250°F (121°C) to 300°F (148°C), fry them for 4-5 minutes or until they become golden brown. Turn them over with a wooden spatula and fry 3-4 minutes more. Remove the gujiya with a slotted spoon and drop them into the sugar water syrup. Soak for 3-4 minutes and then remove them from the syrup.

6. Offer to Lord Krishna.

Mawa Kachori

There is one sweet shop in Jaipur named 'Rawat Mishathan Bhandar' which is very famous for its kachoris. Besides spicy and salty kachoris, this shop also makes and sells sweet mawa kachoris.

Preparation and cooking time: about 1 hour 15 minutes
Makes: 16 pieces

2 cups white flour
¼ cup + 1 tablespoon ghee or unsalted butter
½ cup (120 ml) or as required warm water
¼ cup powdered sugar
1 cup instant, non-fat milk powder
½ cup (120 ml) whole milk
¾ tablespoon charoli (available at Indian grocery stores)
1/3 teaspoon cardamom powder
¼ teaspoon nutmeg
2 cups sugar
¾ cup (180 ml) water
ghee for deep frying

1. Mix the flour and ¼ cup melted ghee or unsalted butter in a mixing bowl. Add enough warm water to make soft dough. Knead well, cover and set aside.

2. Boil the water and sugar in a 3-quart saucepan over medium heat until the sugar dissolves. Raise the heat and boil for 5-7 minutes. Set aside.

3. Melt 1 tablespoon ghee or unsalted butter in a 3 quart saucepan. Stirring constantly, add the milk powder and whole milk and cook for 10-12 minutes or until it turns into a paste.

4. Add the charoli, cardamom powder and nutmeg. Mix well and transfer to a mixing bowl. Cool down and add the powdered sugar. Mix well and set aside.

5. Divide the dough into 16 portions. Shape each portion into a smooth ball. Flatten into a 2½" (6.5 cm) circle. Place about one tablespoon of the mixture in the center of the circle, then bring the sides of the circle over the filling to close it. Pinch the seams together until they're nicely sealed then gently press between your palms to flatten them.

6. Heat the ghee in a 2½" (6.5 cm) deep frying pan over medium heat until the temperature reaches 250°F (121°C). Slip the kachoris into the ghee without crowding them. Slowly fry the kachoris for 12-15 minutes or until they turn golden brown, then turn them over carefully with a wooden spatula. Maintaining a temperature of 250°F (121°C) to 300°F(148°C), fry for 7-8 minutes more or until they become golden brown on both sides. Remove them with a slotted spoon.

7. Drop the kachoris into the sugar syrup and soak for 5-7 minutes, then carefully take them out.

8. Offer to Lord Krishna.

Balushahi

There is one town in Rajasthan named "Kishangarh". This town is very famous for their Rajasthani paintings and balushahi. People specifically go there to buy this sweet.

Preparation and cooking time: about 1 hour 15 minutes
Makes: 24 pieces

4 cups unbleached white flour
1 teaspoon baking powder
½ cup melted ghee or unsalted butter
1 teaspoon cardamom powder
1¼ cups (300 ml) or as required buttermilk
3 cups sugar
1½ cups (360 ml) water
ghee for deep frying
3 tablespoons chopped pistachios

1. Combine the flour, baking powder, melted ghee or butter and cardamom powder in a bowl. Mix well and add enough buttermilk to make soft dough. Divide the dough into 24 portions and roll each one into a ball. The balls should not be very smooth. (Balushahi's texture is supposed to be rough.) Flatten the balls between your palms making sure they are not round. Make a depression in each flat pastry with your thumb; the center

will be thinner than the outer edge. This is the traditional balushahi shape. Transfer these onto a greased baking tray and set them aside.

2. Stirring occasionally, boil the sugar and water in a 3-quart saucepan over medium heat until sugar dissolves. Raise the heat and boil for 5-7 minutes or until the sugar reaches a string-like consistency when poured. Set the sugar syrup aside.

3. Heat the ghee in a 6-quart stockpot until the temperature reaches 215°F (101°C). Slip as many pastries as you can fit into the ghee and fry them for 8-10 minutes or until they become golden brown on one side. Maintain the temperature between 215°F (101°C) to 250°F (121°C) while frying. Turn the pastries over with a wooden spatula and fry them for 7-8 minutes or until they become golden brown.

4. Remove the balushahi from the ghee with a slotted spoon and drop them into the sugar syrup.

5. Remove from the syrup after 4-5 minutes and allow them cool down. Again press the center of the balushahi with your thumb and fill the depression with chopped pistachios.

6. Offer to Lord Krishna.

Shakarpara

This is a traditional Rajasthani sweet which is offered to Sri Sri Radha Govinda Dev Ji in Jaipur.

Preparation and cooking time: about 1 hour 15 minutes
Makes: 24 pieces

3 cups sugar
1½ cups (360 ml) water
2 cups unbleached white flour
¼ cup melted ghee or unsalted butter
½ teaspoon cardamom powder
½ cup (120 ml) or as required warm milk
ghee for deep frying

1. Stirring occasionally, boil the sugar and water in a 3-quart saucepan over medium heat until the sugar dissolves. Raise the heat and boil 7-8 minutes. Set aside.

2. Combine the flour, melted ghee and cardamom powder. Mix well and add enough warm milk to make dough that is firm. Divide the dough into 4 portions and roll each portion into a round shape 1/3" thick.

3. There are several things you can do now. You can cut 6 pieces from each portion with a cookie cutter or use a knife to make your own shapes. You may also divide the dough into 24 portions and roll each portion into a ball, then flatten the balls between your palms. (Usually this shape

shakarpara is offered in the Sri Sri Radha Govinda Dev Ji temple.) Prick the shakarpara all over with a fork so they don't puff during frying.

4. Heat the ghee in a 6-quart stockpot until the temperature reaches 215°F (101°C). Drop the shakarpara into the ghee without crowding them and while maintaining a temperature of 215°F (101°C) to 250°F (121°C). Repeat the same process until all the shakarparas are fried. This will take 12-15 minutes.

5. Remove the shakarpara from the ghee and immediately drop them into the sugar syrup. Soak them for 4-5 minutes and remove.

6. Offer to Lord Krishna.

Besan Ki Chakki

Rajasthani ladies often cook this sweet at home. They store it in a container and offer it immediately to guests when they visit their home. People from Rajasthan also carry this sweet whenever they travel.

Preparation and cooking time: about 1 hour
Makes: 35 pieces

2½ cups sugar
1¾ cups (420 ml) water
2¾ cups ghee or unsalted butter
4 cups besan (chickpea) flour

2 cups instant, non-fat dry milk powder
1¼ teaspoons cardamom powder
¾ teaspoon nutmeg powder
½ teaspoon crushed saffron
2 tablespoons sliced almonds
2 tablespoons sliced pistachios

1. Boil the sugar and water in a 3-quart saucepan over medium heat until the sugar dissolves. Raise the heat and boil about 8-10 minutes more. Take the pan off of the heat and set aside.

2. Melt the ghee or butter in a heavy-bottomed, 6-quart stockpot. Add the chickpea flour and stirring constantly, cook over medium heat for 5 minutes. Turn the heat down to low. Stirring constantly, cook for 10-12 minutes more or until the flour turns light brown. Turn off the heat and add the milk powder, cardamom powder, nutmeg and saffron. Using a whisk, mix well.

3. Pour the sugar syrup slowly into the cooked mixture. Stir constantly until the mixture absorbs the liquid. Transfer the mixture into a greased 9" x 13" x 2" baking pan.

4. Decorate with the almonds and pistachios slices and allow to cool and set for few hours.

5. Cut into squares.

6. Offer to Lord Krishna.

Churma Chakki

One town in Rajasthan named Salasar has a very famous temple of Hanumanji and churma chakki is the main sweet that is offered. Rajasthani people are very devoted to this Hanuman Deity and on Tuesdays and the Purnima, this temple is very crowded.

Preparation and cooking time: about 1 hour
Makes: 35 pieces.

4 cups chickpea flour
½ cup melted ghee or unsalted butter
1 cup (240 ml) (or as required) warm milk
1 cup (240 ml) water
1¾ cups sugar
½ teaspoon cardamom powder
¼ teaspoon saffron
1 cup instant, non-fat dry milk
ghee for deep frying

1. Mix the chickpea flour and melted ghee or unsalted butter in a mixing bowl. Add enough warm milk to make dough that is not too soft and not too firm. Divide the dough into 16-18 portions and roll each portion into a ball. Flatten each ball between your palms.

2. Heat the ghee in a 6-quart stockpot until the temperature reaches 250°F (121°C). Drop the flat patties into the ghee without crowding them and fry them until they become golden brown. Repeat this process while maintaining a temperature of 250°F (121°C) to 300°F (148°C) until all the patties are fried. This will take 8-10 minutes. Remove the fried patties and allow them to cool.

3. Break the fried patties into small pieces. If you feel the patties are not cooked properly on the inside, you can fry them again for 4-5 minutes.

4. Grind them for about 1-2 minutes in the food processor to make a fine mixture. Transfer into a mixing bowl and add the milk powder. Mix well

5. Boil the sugar, water, cardamom powder and saffron in a 3-quart saucepan over medium heat until the sugar is dissolved. Stir occasionally.

6. Raise the heat and boil for 5-6 minutes more.

7. Slowly pour the sugar syrup in the mixture and mix well. Transfer this to a greased "9"x13"x2" baking pan.

8. Allow to cool and set for a few hours. Cut into squares.

9. Offer to Lord Krishna.

Moong Flour Ki Chakki

Rajasthani ladies like to make sweets with yellow split moong dal. For a change, I am using moong flour to cut down on time.

Preparation and cooking time: about 40 minutes
Makes: 35 pieces

1 cup almonds
3½ cups ghee or unsalted butter
4 cups moong flour (available at Indian grocery stores)
2 cups instant, non-fat dry milk powder
3 cups powdered sugar
4 tablespoons sliced almonds

1. Grind the almonds in a food processor and set aside. Melt the ghee or butter in a 6-quart stockpot and add the ground almonds. Cook for 5-6 minutes over medium heat.
2. Add the moong flour and cook for about 5 minutes over medium heat. Turn the heat down to low and cook for 7-8 minutes or until the mixture becomes light brown. Transfer this to a bowl.
3. Add the milk powder and powdered sugar. Mix well. Transfer to a greased 9" x 13" x 2" baking pan and decorate with the sliced almonds.
4. Allow to cool and set for few hours. Cut into squares.
5. Offer to Lord Krishna.

Aate Ki Chakki

Rajasthani ladies use a lot of wheat flour and nuts in their cooking so I was thinking I should try to make some sweet that requires both ingredients. This is one of the sweets that the devotees at New Goloka liked very much.

Preparation and cooking time: about 30 minutes
Makes: 35 pieces

¾ cup pistachios
¾ cup almonds
¾ cup cashews
3 cups ghee or unsalted butter
4 cups chapati or whole wheat flour
2½ cups powdered sugar
3 tablespoons sliced almonds for decoration

1. Grind all the nuts together in a food processor.
2. Melt the ghee or butter in a 6-quart stockpot. Add the nuts and over low heat, stir constantly for 5-7 minutes or until the nuts turn light brown. Turn the heat to medium, add the flour and stir constantly for about 15 minutes or until the flour turns light brown.
3. Transfer this to a mixing bowl. Immediately add the powdered sugar and mix well. Transfer the sweet into a greased 9"x13"x2" baking pan. Decorate with sliced almonds.
4. Allow to cool and set for few hours. Cut into squares.
5. Offer to Lord Krishna.

Note: I usually use chapati flour for this sweet because it's smoother than whole wheat flour, but if you do not have this, then use whole wheat flour.

Amrat Pak

My friend, Vrindavaneshvari mataji, has been living in Vrindavan for the last 10 years and is fully engaged in devotional service. She kindly shared this recipe with me.

Preparation and cooking time: about 40 minutes.
Makes: 35 pieces

½ cup almonds
¾ cup pistachios
2½ cups ghee or unsalted butter
1 cup semolina
1½ cups chickpea flour
1 cup unbleached white flour
1 cup instant, non-fat dry milk
1 cup dried, grated coconut
1½ teaspoons cardamom powder
½ teaspoon saffron powder
¾ teaspoon nutmeg powder
2½ cups powdered sugar

1. Grind the almonds and pistachios in a food processor and set aside.
2. Melt the ghee or butter in a 6-quart stockpot. Add the semolina and stirring constantly, cook over medium heat for 5 minutes. Add the chickpea flour and stir another 5 minutes, then add the white flour. Still stirring, cook for 10 minutes more.
3. Transfer this to a mixing bowl and add the rest of the ingredients. Mix well and transfer into a greased 9" x 13" x 2" baking pan.
4. Allow to cool and set for few hours. Cut into squares.
5. Offer to Lord Krishna.

Almond Simply Wonderfuls

This recipe is inspired by His Divine Grace Srila Prabhupada's personal recipe, 'Simply Wonderfuls.'

Preparation and cooking time: about 30 minutes
Makes: 20 pieces

11/3 cups ghee or unsalted butter
1 cup ground almonds
2 cups instant, non-fat dried milk powder
1¼ cups powdered sugar

1. Melt the ghee or butter in a 3-quart saucepan. Add the ground almonds and cook them for about 2-3 minutes over medium heat or until they become light brown.

2. Transfer to a mixing bowl and allow the mixture to cool for 12-15 minutes. Add the milk powder and powdered sugar. Mix well. Roll into medium-sized balls.

3. Offer to Lord Krishna.

Note: It is important that the cooked almonds be cooled down before you add the milk powder and powdered sugar otherwise there will be crystals in the mixture.

Chaval Ke Sattu

In Rajasthan it is said that Sudama offered this sweet to Lord Krishna and received special mercy. Traditionally, this sweet is made by roasting the rice in a Rajasthani oven named 'bhati', and then by grinding it in a Rajasthani blender named 'chakki' which is made with heavy stones. The ground rice is then mixed with melted ghee and powdered sugar. I am using rice flour to make it easier.

Preparation and cooking time: about 1 hour
Makes: 28 pieces

1¾ cups ghee or unsalted butter
4 cups rice flour
1 teaspoon cardamom powder
2 cups powdered sugar

1. Melt the ghee or butter in a 6-quart stockpot. Add the rice flour and cook it over medium heat for 5 minutes. Turn the heat on low and stir constantly until the flour changes its color. This will take about 15-20 minutes. Add the cardamom powder, transfer it into a mixing bowl and allow it to cool down.
2. Add the powdered sugar and divide the mixture into 28 portions.
3. Roll each portion into a small ball and flatten it in your palm.
4. Offer to Lord Krishna.

Note: I like to decorate this sweet with designs by using food coloring.

Mohan Bhoga

This sweet is similar to the famous South Indian sweet mysor pak. It is easy to make and is a nice preparation to offer to Lord Krishna Who is also named Mohan.

Preparation and cooking time: about 40 minutes
Makes: 20 pieces

1 cup ghee
1 cup chickpea flour
1 cup sugar
1 cup (240 ml) milk
1 cup dried, grated coconut
1 teaspoon cardamom seeds

1. Melt the ghee in a 6-quart stockpot. Add all the ingredients to the ghee and stirring constantly, cook for 12-15 minutes over medium heat. Turn the heat down to low and continuing to stir, cook for 5-7 more minutes.
2. Transfer the mixture to a 11" x 7" x 2" greased baking pan.
3. Allow to cool and set for a few hours. Cut into squares.
4. Offer to Lord Krishna.

Gulgula

This is a traditional Rajasthani sweet pakora. It is offered to the Deities on Govardhana Puja. There is also a tradition in Rajasthan that gulgula is cooked on one of the Saturdays in the month of Kartika, and after offering it to the Deities, it is fed to the animals in the street.

Preparation and cooking time: about 30 minutes
Makes: 32 pieces

1 cup whole wheat flour
¾ cup sugar
½ teaspoon baking powder
¾ cup (180 ml) (or as required) warm water
ghee for deep frying

1. Combine the flour, sugar and baking powder in a bowl. Mix well and add enough warm water to make a thick batter. Cover the bowl and let it sit for 15-20 minutes.

2. Heat the ghee in a 2½" (6.5 cm) deep frying pan until the temperature reaches 250°F (121°C). Take a little mixture (about 1 tablespoon) between your fingers and thumb and drop it carefully into the hot ghee. Drop the gulgulas into the ghee without crowding them.

3. Occasionally moving the gulgulas with a wooden spatula, fry them until they become golden brown, maintaining a temperature of 250°F (121°C) to 300°F (148°C). This will take 10-12 minutes. Remove them with a slotted spoon.

4. Offer the hot gulgula to Lord Krishna.

The Author

Krishna Priya Dasi is a disciple of His Holiness Lokanath Swami. She was born in Rajasthan and raised in Jaipur, India. Jaipur is the capital of Rajasthan and is famous for the Sri Sri Radha Govinda Dev Ji temple.

Although Krishna Priya Dasi encountered major structural and bone problems from the beginning of her life, and underwent major brain surgery in 2005, she continues to cook for Lord Krishna. Besides cooking, she paints traditional Rajasthani art and writes devotional poems. Her poetry book, *Lotus Lyrics*, inspired by His Divine Grace A.C. Bhaktivedanta Swami Prabhupada's *Bhagavad-gita As It Is*, has received much appreciation. One of her paintings, *Rasa-Lila*, which she painted with help of artist Mohan Soni in Jaipur, is printed on the front cover of *Dance of Divine Love* by Graham M. Schweig. She has been cooking for Sri Sri Radha Golokananda at New Goloka, NC USA since 1996.

Cooking for Krishna

by Krishna Priya Dasi

Cooking for Krishna brings happiness -
We all seek this most-wanted treasure.
Our good fortune increases without limit
When we please the source of all pleasure.

Cooking for Krishna is a matchless gift
Which fulfills all of our dreams.
Our senses become gratified
Once we satisfy the Supreme.

Cooking for Krishna is the stream of nectar
That quenches our thirst for fulfillment.
We no longer feel so desert-like
And feel no more discontentment.

Cooking for Krishna is ever-inspiring,
And lifts us to the realm of transcendence.
This devotional service will always bestow
Deep satisfaction and self-confidence.

Cooking for Krishna is a great benediction,
A blessing by Srila Prabhupada's grace.
Our relationship becomes firm with the Lord;
Pure and deep realization takes place.